Man

MW00883423

Mike Busch A&P/IA

A Revolutionary Approach to General Aviation Maintenance

To my wife Jan, love of my life, best friend, and steadfast companion for four decades: Your support, encouragement, and sustenance enabled me to live my life in hot pursuit of one exciting and fulfilling challenge after another.

P.S. Kindly do not predecease me as I cannot imagine living without you, and I'll be damned if I can remember how I managed before we met.

To my maintenance mentors Tom Carr, Steve Ells, John Frank, Bruce Hatch, Phil Kirkham, Paul New, Jimmy Tubbs, Dan Volberding, and the late Bob Mosley and Tom Rogers: I can never repay your generosity, wisdom, patience, and kindness in mentoring me from know-nothing nugget to A&P/IA to National Aviation Maintenance Technician of the Year, so I'll do my best to pay it forward by mentoring the next generation of GA mechanics and maintenance-savvy aircraft owners.

Table of Contents

Prologue

This book is the first of a multivolume set. I decided to create these books to anthologize and preserve the hundreds of magazine and e-zine articles and blog posts I've written over the past two decades on a wide variety of general aviation (GA) topics, mostly maintenance-related. The remaining volumes in this set will be devoted to engines, airframes, ownership, and flying. Each will be an anthology of my most important articles on those subjects.

This book is different. It's shorter, pithier, and largely devoid of the war stories and nuts-and-bolts discussions that characterize most of my articles. Its purpose is to articulate my philosophy of aircraft maintenance and ownership, a philosophy that permeates all of my writing and speaking, and the credo that underlies my business activities—SavvyAviator, SavvyAnalysis, SavvyPrebuy, SavvyMx. Hence its "Manifesto" title.

The maintenance philosophy I articulate here is admittedly controversial in GA maintenance circles despite the fact that it's universally accepted in most other segments of aviation, including air transport, military, and bizjets. Maintenance of owner-flown

GA aircraft is still done largely the same way it was done in the 1950s and 1960s. My goal is to help drag it—kicking and screaming—into the 21st century. If that makes me an iconoclast, so be it.

What's in This Book

My manifesto begins with some history lessons about the origins of modern aviation maintenance philosophy. It discusses the pioneering work of Professor C.H. Waddington and his team of scientists attached to the Royal Air Force (RAF) Coastal Command in the early 1940s, who were responsible for dramatically increasing the reliability and force-readiness of the RAF's B-24 bomber fleet by slashing the amount of preventive maintenance performed on them. I then fast-forward to the late 1960s and the groundbreaking work of scientists Stan Nowlan and Howard Heap at United Airlines, who independently rediscovered Waddington's findings and took them to the next level by defining the fundamental principles of reliability-centered maintenance (RCM). Their work became the very foundation of modern maintenance practices employed by virtually every segment of aviation—with the sole exception of owner-flown GA.

Next, I address piston aircraft engines, specifically the misguided practice of overhauling them at fixed time-between-overhaul (TBO) intervals. I discuss the research of Dr. Nathan Ulrich, which analyzed the relationship between engine-failure accidents and engine time, and demonstrates clearly that the greatest risk of catastrophic engine failure is when the engine is young, not when it's old. I make a case for ignoring recommended TBOs and maintaining and overhauling engines strictly on-condition, something the airlines have been doing for nearly 50 years. I offer detailed suggestions about how such condition monitoring should be done—with emphasis on modern condition-monitoring technologies like borescopy, digital engine monitor data analysis and scanning electron microscopy—and how the decision when to overhaul should be made.

I then turn to aviation maintenance's "dirty little secret" that nobody likes to talk about: Mechanics sometimes break airplanes while attempting to fix them. Years ago I coined a term for such events: "maintenance-induced failures" (MIFs). They're a far larger problem than most people think, accounting for one out of eight aircraft accidents and a large share of mechanical problems. MIFs are precisely why first Waddington and later Nowlan and Heap discovered that the best way to make aircraft more reliable is to do *less* maintenance on them. MIFs are precisely the reason I am an unabashed and outspoken maintenance minimalist.

I discuss how most A&Ps think, and why. Most GA mechanics are trained as maintenance maximalists. They genuinely believe that more maintenance is better (even though the data proves that it's worse). Most are reluctant to try new products or technologies or to depart from traditional maintenance methods or manufacturer recommendations for fear of being sued; I call this "defensive maintenance," and it's every bit as pernicious a problem as "defensive medicine" is in healthcare.

My next focus is on the responsibility that GA owners have for airworthiness and maintenance. I argue that owners need to make their own well-informed maintenance decisions, not abdicate those decisions to their mechanics. I call this concept "owner-in-command" because it parallels the "pilot-in-command" concept that we all learned as student pilots. This Manifesto goes into some detail about the steps an owner-in-command should take to remain in control of the maintenance of his aircraft, and why simply rubber-stamping a mechanic's maintenance recommendations could be hazardous to an owner's health as well as his wallet.

Finally, I point out that the first flight after any maintenance—whether a heavy annual or a routine oil change—is always the most likely time for a mechanical failure to occur. Owners should religiously perform a post-maintenance test flight without passengers, in VMC, close to the airport, and (most importantly) with a test pilot's mindset. This flight is the owner's last defense against MIFs, and another responsibility that an owner must never shirk.

Acknowledgements

This book wouldn't exist without the enthusiastic encouragement and persistent prodding of my trusted consiglieri Adam Smith and Chris Wrather; the many merciless excisions by my awesome editor Mary Jones (EditEtc LLC), without whom this book would be twice as wordy and half as pithy; and the consummate skill of my graphic designer Lynn Stuart (Lynn Stuart Graphic Design), who miraculously managed to make me look good in print. But I wrote and proofread this Manifesto myself, so responsibility for errors or offenses herein is mine and mine alone.

—Michael D. Busch, July 2014

1

The Waddington Effect

Maintenance isn't an inherently good thing (like exercise);
it's a necessary evil (like surgery)

In 1943, a British scientist named Conrad Hal (C.H.) Waddington made a remarkable discovery about aircraft maintenance. He was a most unlikely person to make this discovery because he wasn't an aeronautical engineer, an aircraft mechanic, or even a pilot. He was a gifted developmental biologist, paleontologist, geneticist, embryologist, philosopher, poet, and painter who was not particularly interested in aviation. But like many other British scientists at that time, his career was interrupted by the outbreak of World War II, and he found himself pressed into service with the Royal Air Force (RAF).

C.H. Waddington (1905–1975)

Waddington wound up reporting to the RAF Coastal Command, heading up a group of fellow scientists in its Operational Research Section. Their job was to advise the British military on how to combat the threat from German submarines more effectively. In that capacity, Waddington and his colleagues developed a series of astonishing recommendations that defied military conventional wisdom of the time.

For example, the bombers used to hunt and sink U-boats were mostly painted black to make them difficult to see. But Waddington's group ran a series of experiments that proved that bombers painted white were not spotted by the U-boats until they were 20 percent closer, resulting in a 30-percent increase in successful sinkings. Waddington's group also recommended that the depth charges dropped by the bombers be set to explode at a depth of 25 feet instead of 100 feet. This recommendation—initially resisted by RAF commanders—ultimately resulted in a sevenfold increase in the number of U-boats destroyed.

These guys were really smart!

Waddington subsequently turned his attention to the problem of "force readiness" of the bombers. The Coastal Command's B-24 Liberator bombers were spending an inordinate amount of time in the maintenance shop instead of hunting U-boats. In July 1943, the two British Liberator squadrons located at Ballykelly,

Northern Ireland, consisted of 40 aircraft, but at any given time only about 20 were flight-ready. The other aircraft were down for any number of reasons, but mostly undergoing maintenance or waiting for parts.

A Consolidated B-24 Liberator in RAF service.

At the time, conventional wisdom held that if more preventive maintenance (PM) was performed on each aircraft, fewer problems would arise and more incipient problems would be caught and fixed—and thus fleet readiness would surely improve.

Conventional wisdom was wrong. It would take Dr. Waddington and his Operational Research team to prove just how wrong.

Waddington and his team started gathering data about the scheduled and unscheduled maintenance of these aircraft and began crunching and analyzing the numbers. When he plotted the number of unscheduled aircraft repairs as a function of flight time, Waddington discovered something both unexpected and significant: The number of unscheduled breakdowns (i.e., squawks) spiked sharply right after each aircraft underwent its regular 50-hour scheduled maintenance, and then declined steadily over time until the next scheduled 50-hour maintenance, at which time they spiked up once again.

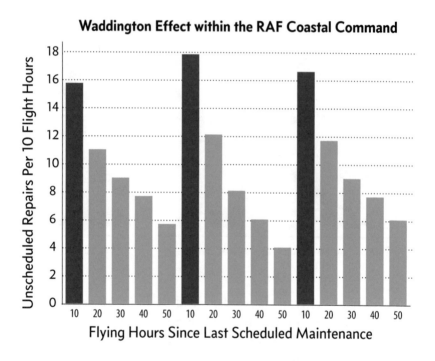

Waddington Effect within the RAF Coastal Command

The number of squawks spiked after each scheduled 50-hour preventive maintenance (PM) cycle, and then declined until the next 50-hour PM cycle. Clearly the PM was doing more harm than good.

When Waddington examined the plot of this repair data, he concluded that the scheduled maintenance (in Waddington's own words) "tends to INCREASE breakdowns, and this can only be because it is doing positive harm by disturbing a relatively satisfactory state of affairs. There is no sign that the rate of breakdowns is starting to increase again after 40–50 flying hours when the aircraft is coming due for its next scheduled maintenance."

In other words, the observed pattern of unscheduled breakdowns demonstrated that the scheduled preventive maintenance was actually doing more harm than good, and that the 50-hour preventive maintenance interval was inappropriately short.

The solution proposed by Waddington's team—and ultimately accepted by the RAF commanders over the howls of their maintenance personnel—was to increase the time interval between scheduled maintenance cycles and to eliminate all preventive maintenance tasks that couldn't be proven to be demonstrably beneficial. Once these recommendations were implemented, the number of effective flying hours of the RAF Coastal Command bomber fleet increased by a whopping 60 percent!

Takeaway: Maintenance isn't an inherently good thing (like exercise); it's a necessary evil (like surgery). We have to do it from time to time, but we sure don't want to do more than absolutely necessary to keep our aircraft safe and reliable. Doing more maintenance than necessary actually degrades safety and reliability instead of enhancing it.

2
The Roots of Reliability-Centered Maintenance

The optimal maintenance strategy for most aircraft components is simply to leave them alone, wait until they fail, and then replace or repair them when they do.

Fast forward two decades to the 1960s, when a pair of gifted scientists at United Airlines—aeronautical engineer Stanley Nowlan and mathematician Howard Heap—independently rediscovered these principles in their pioneering research on optimizing maintenance. They were almost certainly unaware of the work of C.H. Waddington and his colleagues in Britain in the 1940s because that work remained classified until 1973, when Waddington's meticulously kept diary of his wartime research activities was declassified and published.

Nowlan and Heap independently rediscovered the utter wrong-headedness of traditional scheduled preventive maintenance, and took things to the next level by formulating a rigorous engineering technique for creating optimal maintenance programs to maximize safety and dispatch reliability while minimizing cost and downtime. **Their methodology became known as "reliability-centered maintenance" (RCM),** and it revolutionized the way maintenance is done in the airline industry, military aviation, high-end bizjets, space flight, and numerous non-aviation applications from nuclear power plants to auto factories.

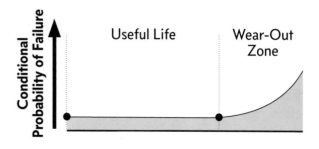

The traditional approach to PM assumes that most components start out reliable, and then at some point become unreliable as they age

The "Useful Life" Fallacy

Nowlan and Heap proved the fallaciousness of two fundamental principles underlying traditional scheduled PM:

- Components start off being reliable, but their reliability deteriorates with age.

- The useful life of components can be established statistically, so components can be retired or overhauled before they fail.

It turns out that both of these principles are wrong. To quote Nowlan and Heap:

> One of the underlying assumptions of maintenance theory has always been that there is a fundamental cause-and-effect relationship between scheduled maintenance and operating reliability. **This assumption was based on the intuitive belief that because mechanical parts wear out, the reliability of any equipment is directly related to operating age.** It therefore followed that the more frequently equipment was overhauled, the better protected it was against the likelihood of failure. The only problem was in determining what age limit was necessary to assure reliable operation.

> In the case of aircraft, it was also commonly assumed that all reliability problems were directly related to operating safety. Over the years, however, it was found that many types of failures could not be prevented no matter how intensive the maintenance activities. [Aircraft] designers were able to cope with this problem, not by preventing failures, but by preventing such failures from affecting safety. In most aircraft, essential functions are protected by redundancy features which ensure that, in the event of a failure, the necessary function will still be available from some other source.

> **Despite the time-honored belief that reliability was directly related to the intervals between scheduled overhauls, searching studies based on actuarial analysis of failure data suggested that the traditional hard-time policies were, apart from their expense, ineffective in controlling failure rates.**

This was not because the intervals were not short enough, and surely not because the tear down inspections were not sufficiently thorough. Rather, it was because, contrary to expectations, for many items the likelihood of failure did not in fact increase with increasing age. Consequently a maintenance policy based exclusively on some maximum operating age would, no matter what the age limit, have little or no effect on the failure rate. [1,2]

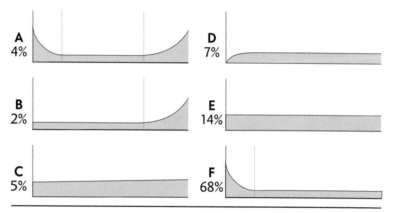

RCM researchers found that only 2 percent of aircraft components have failures that are predominantly age-related (curve B), and that 68 percent have failures that are primarily infant mortality (curve F).

Winning the War by Picking our Battles

Another traditional maintenance fallacy is the intuitive notion that aircraft component failures are dangerous and need to be prevented through PM. A major focus of RCM was to identify the ways that various components fail, and then evaluate the frequency and consequences of those failures. This is known as Failure Modes and

1. [F. Stanley Nowlan and Howard F. Heap, "Reliability-Centered Maintenance" 1978, DoD Report Number AD-A066579.]
2. Bold emphasis is that of this book's author, not Nowlan and Heap.

Effects Analysis (FMEA). Researchers found that while certain failure modes have serious consequences that can compromise safety (e.g., a cracked wing spar), the overwhelming majority of component failures have no safety impact and have consequences that are quite acceptable (e.g., a failed #2 comm radio or #3 hydraulic pump). **Under the RCM philosophy, it makes no sense whatsoever to perform PM on components whose failure has acceptable consequences; the optimal maintenance approach for such components is simply to leave them alone, wait until they fail, and then replace or repair them when they do.** This strategy is known as "run to failure" and is a major tenet of RCM.

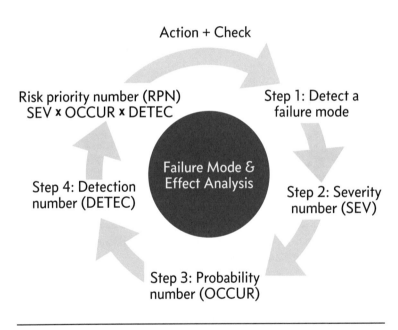

Failure Mode & Effects Analysis (FMEA) evaluates the risk associated with various failure modes. It considers three factors: (1) how severe the consequences of the failure are, (2) how likely the failure is to occur, and (3) how difficult it is to detect the failure while it's still incipient.

A Maintenance Revolution

The work of Nowlan and Heap revolutionized maintenance practices in the airline industry. RCM-inspired maintenance programs were developed for the Boeing 747, Douglas DC-10, and Lockheed L-1011, and for all subsequent airliners. The contrast between the traditional (pre-RCM) maintenance programs for the Boeing 707 and 727 and Douglas DC-8 was astonishing. The vast majority of component time-between-overhauls (TBOs) and life-limits were abandoned in favor of an on-condition approach based on monitoring the actual condition of engines and other components and keeping them in service until their condition demonstrably deteriorated to an unacceptable degree.

The 747, shown here, DC-10 and L-1011 were the first airliners that had RCM-based maintenance programs.

For example, the DC-8 had 339 components with TBOs or life limits, whereas the DC-10 had only seven—and none of them were engines. (Research showed clearly that overhauling engines at a specific TBO didn't make them safer and actually did the opposite.)

The amount of scheduled maintenance was drastically reduced. For example, the DC-8 maintenance program required 4,000,000 labor hours of major structural inspections during the aircraft's first 20,000 hours in service, while the 747 maintenance program called for only 66,000 labor hours—a reduction of nearly two orders of magnitude.

Of course, these changes saved the airlines a king's ransom in reduced maintenance costs and scheduled downtime. At the same time, the airplanes had far fewer maintenance squawks and much better dispatch reliability.

Takeaway: Everything that the airlines learned from the research of Nowlan and Heap applies equally to owner-flown GA: Most aircraft components are not safety-critical and should be run to failure. Most safety-critical components are far more likely to fail when they're young than when they're old and should be maintained strictly on-condition, not on a fixed timetable.

3

Do Piston Engine TBOs Make Sense?

Despite an overwhelming body of scientific research demonstrating that time-based preventive maintenance is counterproductive, worthless, unnecessary, wasteful, and incredibly costly, we're still doing it. Why?

Today, there's only one segment of aviation that has not adopted the enlightened RCM approach to maintenance and still does scheduled PM the dumb, old-fashioned way. Sadly, that segment is owner-flown general aviation (GA) aircraft—particularly piston-powered GA aircraft—at the bottom of the aviation food chain where a lot of us hang out. Even now, in the 21st century, maintenance of piston aircraft remains largely time-based rather than condition-based.

Most owners of piston GA aircraft dutifully overhaul their engines at TBO, overhaul their propellers every 5 to 7 years, and replace their alternators and vacuum pumps every 500 hours just as

Continental, Lycoming, Hartzell, McCauley, HET and Parker Aerospace advise. Many Bonanza and Baron owners have their wing bolts pulled every 5 years, and most Cirrus owners have their batteries replaced every 2 years for no good reason (other than that it's in the manufacturer's maintenance manual).

Despite an overwhelming body of scientific research demonstrating that time-based preventive maintenance is counterproductive, worthless, unnecessary, and incredibly costly, we're still doing it. Why?

Mostly, I think, because of fear of litigation. Manufacturers are afraid to change anything for fear of being sued (because if they change anything, it could be construed to mean that what they were doing before was wrong). Shops and mechanics are afraid to deviate from what the manufacturers recommend for fear of being sued (because they deviated from manufacturers' guidance).

Let's face it: Neither the manufacturers nor the maintainers have any real incentive to change. The cost of doing all this counterproductive, worthless, unnecessary, and wasteful preventive maintenance (that actually doesn't prevent anything) is not coming out of their pockets; it's going into their pockets!

If we're going to drag piston GA maintenance kicking and screaming into the 21st century, it's going to have to be aircraft owners who force the change. Owners are the ones with the incentive to change the way things are being done. Owners are the ones who can exert power over the manufacturers and maintainers by voting with their feet and their credit cards.

For this to happen, owners of piston GA aircraft need to understand the best way to do maintenance—the RCM way. Then they need to direct their shops and mechanics to maintain their aircraft that way, or take their maintenance business to someone who will. This means that owners need both knowledge and courage.

When is a Piston Aircraft Engine Most Likely to Hurt You?

Fifty years ago, RCM researchers proved conclusively that overhauling turbine engines at a fixed TBO is counterproductive, and that engine overhauls should be done strictly on-condition. But how can we be sure that this also applies to piston aircraft engines?

In a perfect world, Continental and Lycoming would study this issue and publish their findings. But their attorneys won't let that happen. Continental and Lycoming have consistently refused to release any data on engine failure history of their engines, and likewise they have consistently refused to explain how they arrive at the TBOs they publish. For years, one aggressive plaintiff lawyer after another has tried to compel Continental and Lycoming to answer these questions in court. All have failed miserably.

So if we're going to get answers to these critical questions, we're going to have to rely on engine failure data that we can get our hands on. The most obvious source of such data is the National Transportation Safety Board (NTSB) accident database. That's precisely what brilliant mechanical engineer Nathan T. Ulrich, Ph.D., of Lee, New Hampshire, did in 2007. Dr. Ulrich was also a U.S. Coast Guard Auxiliary (USCGA) pilot who was unhappy that USCGA policy forbade him from flying volunteer search-and-rescue missions if his Bonanza's engine was past TBO.

Dr. Ulrich analyzed five years' worth of NTSB accident data for the period 2001–2005 inclusive, examining all accidents involving small piston-powered airplanes (under 12,500 pounds gross weight) for which the NTSB identified "engine failure" as either the probable cause or a contributing factor. From this population of accidents, Dr. Ulrich eliminated those involving air-race and agricultural-application aircraft. Then he analyzed the relationship between the frequency of engine-failure accidents and the number of hours on each engine since it was last built, rebuilt, or overhauled. He did a similar analysis based on the calendar age of the engine. The histograms on the facing page summarize the results of his study.

If these histograms have a vaguely familiar look, it might be because they look an awful lot like the histograms generated by British scientist C.H. Waddington in 1943 that we saw in Chapter 1.

Now, we have to be careful about how we interpret Dr. Ulrich's findings. Ulrich would be the first to admit that NTSB accident data can't tell us much about the risk of engine failures beyond TBO simply because most piston aircraft engines are voluntarily euthanized at or near TBO. So it shouldn't be surprising that we don't see very many engine failure accidents involving engines significantly past TBO since there are so few of them flying. (The engines on my Cessna 310 are at more than 200 percent of TBO, but there just aren't a lot of RCM true believers like me in the piston GA community... yet.)

What Dr. Ulrich's research demonstrates unequivocally is the striking and disturbing frequency of "infant-mortality" engine-failure accidents during the first few years and first few hundred hours after an engine is built, rebuilt, or overhauled. Ulrich's findings make it indisputably clear that by far the most likely time for you to fall out of the sky due to a catastrophic engine failure is when the engine is young, not when it's old. (The next most likely time for you to fall out of the sky is shortly after invasive engine maintenance in the field, particularly cylinder replacement, and I'll talk about that in Chapter 6.)

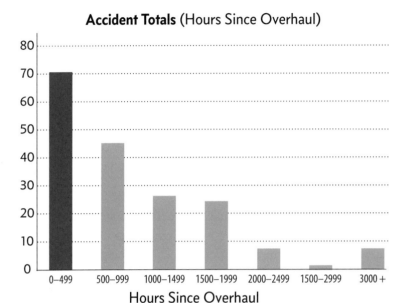

Accident Totals (Hours Since Overhaul)

Hours Since Overhaul

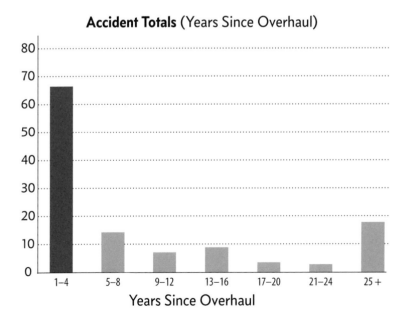

Accident Totals (Years Since Overhaul)

Years Since Overhaul

So…Why Overhaul at TBO?

It doesn't take a rocket scientist (or a Ph.D. in mechanical engineering) to figure out what all this means. If your engine reaches TBO and still gives every indication of being healthy—good performance, not making metal, decent oil analysis and borescope results, etc.—overhauling it will clearly degrade safety, not enhance it. That's simply because it will convert your low-risk old engine into a high-risk young engine. I don't know about you, but that certainly strikes me as a dumb thing to do.

There are several reasons that TBO is a flawed concept. One is that engine life has very little to do with engine hours in service. Hours are not what limit the life of our engines. The biggest life-limiting factor is exposure to corrosive environments during periods of disuse. The next biggest is operator abuse, particularly cold starts and improper powerplant management. None of these factors are reflected in the manufacturer's published TBO.

Why euthanize a healthy engine just because the hour meter rolled over to some fixed value?

Does it make any sense at all that the engine on an aircraft tied down outdoors in Tampa would have the same TBO as one hangared in Tucson? Or that one that flies 400 hours a year would have the same TBO as one that flies 40 hours a year? Or that one that flies mostly long-distance cross-country missions would have the same TBO as one used primarily for flight training?

Of course not! The whole notion of a one-size-fits-all TBO is inherently nonsensical.

So why is overhauling on-condition such a tough sell to our mechanics and the engine manufacturers? The counter-argument goes something like this: "Since we have so little data about the reliability of past-TBO engines (because most engines are arbitrarily euthanized at TBO), how can we be sure that it's safe to operate them beyond TBO?" RCM researchers refer to this as the "Resnikoff Conundrum" (after mathematician H.L. Resnikoff), which states simply that in order to collect failure data we have to allow equipment to fail.

To me, it looks an awful lot like the same circular argument that was used for decades to justify arbitrarily forcing airline pilots to retire at age 60, despite the fact that aeromedical experts were unanimous that this policy made no sense whatsoever. Think about it.

Takeaway: The traditional concept of fixed-interval TBOs is counterproductive and discredited by scientific research. Piston aircraft engines are most likely to fail when they're young, not when they're old. Old engines should be allowed to remain in service as long as they're healthy and should be overhauled or replaced only when they get sick enough to justify accepting the infant-mortality risk of a young engine.

4
What Makes an Engine Airworthy?

Avoid getting preoccupied with things like compression readings and oil consumption that have relatively little correlation with true airworthiness.

If we're going to challenge the traditional practice of automatically overhauling an engine at TBO, how do we assess whether a piston aircraft engine continues to be airworthy and when it's time to do an on-condition overhaul? Compression tests and oil consumption are only part of the story—a smaller part than most owners and mechanics think.

My late friend Bob Moseley was far too humble to call himself a guru, but he knew as much about piston aircraft engines as anyone I've ever met. That's not surprising because he overhauled Continental and Lycoming engines for four decades; there's not much about these engines that he hadn't seen, done, and learned.

James Robert "Bob" Moseley
(1948-2011)

Between 1993 and 1998, "Mose" (as his friends called him) worked for Continental Motors as a field technical representative. He was an airframe and powerplant mechanic (A&P) with inspection authorization (IA) and a FAA-designated airworthiness representative (DAR). He was generous to a fault when it came to sharing his expertise. In that vein, he was a frequent presenter at annual IA renewal seminars.

Which Engine Is Airworthy?

During these seminars, Mose would often challenge a roomful of hundreds of A&P/IA mechanics with a hypothetical scenario that went something like this:

Four good-looking fellows, coincidentally all named Bob, are hanging out at the local Starbucks near the airport one morning, enjoying their usual cappuccinos and biscotti. Remarkably enough, all four Bobs own identical Bonanzas, all with Continental IO-550 engines. Even more remarkable, all four engines have identical calendar times and operating hours.

While sipping their overpriced coffees, the four Bobs start comparing notes. Bob One brags that his engine only uses one quart of oil between 50-hour oil changes, and his compressions are all 75/80 or better. Bob Two says his engine uses a quart every 18 hours, and his compressions are in the low 60s. Bob Three says his engine uses a quart every 8 hours and his compressions are in the high 50s. Bob Four says his compressions are in the low 50s and he adds a quart every 4 hours.

Who has the best engine? And why?

This invariably provoked a vigorous discussion among the IAs. One faction typically thought that Bob One's engine was best. Another usually opined that Bobs Two and Three had the best engines, and that the ultra-low oil consumption of Bob One's engine was indicative of insufficient upper cylinder lubrication and a likely precursor to premature cylinder wear. All the IAs agreed Bob Four's was worst.

Don't place too much emphasis on compression test readings as a measure of engine airworthiness. An engine can have low compression readings while continuing to run smoothly and reliably and make full power to TBO and beyond. Oil consumption is an even less important factor. As long as you don't run out of oil before you run out of fuel, you're fine.

Mose took the position that with nothing more than the given information about compression readings and oil consumption, he considered all four engines equally airworthy. While many people think that ultra-low oil consumption may correlate with accelerated cylinder wear, Continental's research doesn't bear this out, and Mose knew of some engines that went to TBO with very low oil consumption all the way to the end.

While the low compressions and high oil consumption of Bob Four's engine might suggest impending cylinder problems, Mose said that in his experience engines that exhibit a drop in compression and increase in oil consumption after several hundred hours may still make TBO without cylinder replacement. "There's a Twin Bonanza that I take care of, one of whose engines lost compression within the first 300 hours after overhaul," Mose once told me. "The engine is now at 900 hours and the best cylinder measures around 48/80. But the powerplant is running smooth, making full rated power, no leaks, and showing all indications of being a happy engine. It has never had a cylinder off, and I see no reason it shouldn't make TBO."

Lesson of a Lawn Mower

To put these issues of compression and oil consumption in perspective, Mose liked to tell the IAs a story of an engine that was not from Continental or Lycoming but from Briggs & Stratton:

> Years ago, I had a Snapper lawn mower with an 8 horsepower Briggs on it. I purchased it used, so I don't know anything about its prior history. But it ran good, and I used and abused it for about four years, mowing three acres of very hilly, rough ground every summer.
>
> The fifth year I owned this mower, the engine started using oil. By the end of the summer, it was using about 1/2 quart in two hours of mowing. If I wasn't careful, I could run out of oil before I ran out of gas, because the sump only held about a quart when full. The engine still ran great, mowed like new, although it did smoke a little each time I started it.

The sixth year, things got progressively worse, just as you might expect. By the end of the summer, it was obvious that this engine was getting really tired. It still ran okay, would pull the hills, and would mow at the same speed if the grass wasn't too tall. But it got to the point that it was using a quart of oil every hour, and was becoming quite difficult to start. The compression during start was so low (essentially nil) that sometimes I had to spray ether into the carb to get the engine to start. It also started leaking combustion gases around the head bolts, and would blow bubbles if I sprayed soapy water on the head while it was running. In fact, the mower became somewhat useful as a fogger for controlling mosquitoes. But it still made power and would only foul its spark plug a couple of times during the season when things got really bad.

If this one-cylinder engine can perform well while using a quart of oil an hour, surely an aircraft engine with 50 times the displacement can, too.

Now keep in mind that this engine was rated at just 8 horsepower and had just one cylinder with displacement roughly the size of a coffee cup, was using one quart of oil per hour, and had zilch compression. Compare that to an IO-550 with six cylinders, each with a 5.25-inch bore. Do you suppose that oil consumption of one quart per hour or compression of 40/80 would have any measurable effect on an IO-550's power output or reliability—in other words, its airworthiness? Not likely.

In fact, Continental actually ran a dynamometer test on an IO-550 whose compression ring gaps had been filed oversize to intentionally reduce compression on all cylinders to 40/80, and it made full rated power.

Let's Use Common Sense

I really like Mose's commonsense approach to aircraft engines. Whether we're owners or mechanics (or both), we would do well to avoid getting preoccupied with arbitrary measurements like compression readings and oil consumption that have relatively little correlation with true airworthiness.

Instead, we should focus on the stuff that's really important: Is the engine "making metal"? Are there any cracks in the cylinder heads or crankcase? Any exhaust leaks, fuel leaks, or serious oil leaks? Most importantly, does the engine seem to be running rough or falling short of making full rated power?

If the answer to all of those questions is no, then we can be reasonably sure that our engine is airworthy and we can fly behind it with well-deserved confidence.

On-Condition Maintenance

The smart way to deal with engine maintenance—including deciding when to overhaul—is to do it "on-condition" rather than on a fixed timetable. This means that we use all available condition-monitoring tools to monitor the engine's health, and let the engine itself tell us when maintenance is required. This is how the airlines and military have been doing it for decades.

For our piston aircraft engines, we have a marvelous multiplicity of condition-monitoring tools at our disposal.

They include:

- Oil filter visual inspection
- Oil filter scanning electron microscopy (SEM)
- Spectrographic oil analysis programs (SOAP)
- Digital engine monitor data analysis
- Borescope inspection
- Differential compression test
- Visual crankcase inspection
- Visual cylinder head inspection
- Oil consumption trend analysis
- Oil pressure trend analysis

If we use all these tools on an appropriately frequent basis and understand how to interpret the results, we can be confident that we know whether the engine is healthy or not—and if not, what kind of maintenance action is necessary to restore it to health.

Digital borescopes and digital engine monitors have revolutionized condition monitoring of piston aircraft engines.

The moment you abandon the TBO concept and decide to make your maintenance decisions on-condition, you take on an obligation to use these tools—all of them—and pay close attention to what they're telling you. Unfortunately, many owners and mechanics don't understand how to use these tools appropriately or to interpret the results properly.

When Is It Time to Overhaul?

It takes something pretty serious before I conclude it's time to send the engine off to an engine shop for teardown—or to replace it with an exchange engine. Here's a list of the sort of findings that would prompt me to recommend that "the time has come":

- An unacceptably large quantity of visible metal in the oil filter; unless the quantity is very large, we'll often wait until we've seen metal in the filter for several shortened oil-change intervals and verified that it's getting worse, not better.

- A crankcase crack that exceeds acceptable limits, particularly if it's leaking oil.

- A serious oil leak (e.g., at the crankcase parting seam) that cannot be corrected without splitting the case.

- An obviously unairworthy condition observed via direct visual inspection (e.g., a bad cam lobe observed during cylinder or lifter removal).

Badly damaged cam lobe found during cylinder removal.
"It's time!"

- A prop strike, serious overspeed, or other similar event that clearly requires a teardown inspection in accordance with engine manufacturer's guidance.

Takeaway: Ignore TBO, maintain your engine on-condition, make sure you use all the available condition-monitoring tools, make sure you know how to interpret the results (or consult with someone who does), and don't overreact to a single bad oil report or a little metal in the filter. Using this reliability-centered approach to engine maintenance, I've helped thousands of aircraft owners obtain the maximum useful life from their engines, saving them a great deal of money, downtime and hassle. And I haven't had one fall out of the sky yet.

5

Show Me the Data!

The best way to diagnose an engine problem is usually in the air, not on the ground.

"My engine started running rough about halfway home yesterday so I dropped it off at the service center. Could you please work with my mechanic to troubleshoot this problem?"

Arggghhh!!!

Many aircraft owners have a knee-jerk reaction to put their airplane in the shop whenever problems arise. Apparently they assume that diagnosing the problem is the job of a mechanic. That's like having a bellyache and making an appointment to see a surgeon.

Like surgeons, aircraft mechanics are primarily in the business of fixing things that aren't working properly. But before you go to a surgeon or a mechanic, you need to figure out what's wrong. You need a diagnosis.

Every diagnosis starts with data. If you were feeling unwell, the initial data would probably come from a clinical interview (Q&A session) with your primary care physician. The result of that interview would be a detailed, written account of your symptoms. Additional tests—blood work, electrocardiogram, imaging studies, needle biopsy, etc.—might be ordered to gather additional data to refine and confirm the diagnosis.

Similarly, if your aircraft engine seems unwell, the initial data would typically come from your detailed account of its symptoms ("squawks") and a dump of digital engine monitor data. Additional tests—oil and oil filter analysis, compression test, borescope inspection, etc.—might be necessary to gather additional data to refine and confirm the diagnosis.

If you can't analyze your engine monitor data, you'll need to send it to someone who knows how. Sadly, few mechanics have any training or experience in doing this.

If you don't have a digital engine monitor, you're seriously handicapped because you can't take your engine's vital signs. If you do have one but you can't analyze your engine monitor data, you'll probably need to send it to someone who knows how. Sadly, few mechanics have any training or experience in doing this.

If the mechanic's role is that of a surgeon, the aircraft owner's role is that of primary care physician. It is up to you to observe critically and document carefully your engine's symptoms, and to download your digital engine monitor data and analyze it—or to have it professionally analyzed. Very few mechanics have any training or experience in analyzing digital engine monitor data, oil analysis reports, scanning electron microscope findings, etc. (This is something that hopefully will change gradually as mechanic training is dragged kicking and screaming into the 21st century.)

The Owner as Test Pilot

The engine's symptoms obviously must be observed and documented while the aircraft is airborne. Engine monitor data must also be captured in the air. Putting the airplane in the shop terminates any opportunity to do these things, so it's always a mistake to hand the aircraft over to a mechanic too early. Only the grossest and most obvious problems—like an oil leak or a dead magneto—can be diagnosed in the maintenance hangar or during ground runs. Most of the time, the responsibility for gathering the data required to diagnose the problem accurately will most likely fall upon you as owner and pilot, not upon your mechanic. Like it or not, you are a test pilot.

Typically when an aircraft owner asks me for help diagnosing an engine problem, the first thing I ask him or her to do is to fly the airplane and conduct one or more flight-test profiles, then dump the engine monitor data for me to analyze. Eventually, I hope owners learn to conduct the flight-test profiles at the first sign of engine trouble (without me having to ask), eliminating the need for a separate test flight.

The most useful of these flight-test profiles include the ignition stress test and the mixture distribution test.

Ignition Stress Test

Also known as the in-flight lean of peak (LOP) mag check, the ignition stress test is the best way to evaluate the performance of your engine's ignition system. Every student pilot is taught to perform a mag check during the pre-takeoff engine run-up. What they aren't taught is that the standard pre-takeoff mag check can detect only the grossest ignition system defects, such as a fouled spark plug or a dead magneto. You see, it's easy to ignite a rich mixture when the engine is running at relatively low power. So even a mediocre ignition system can get a passing grade.

The higher the power and the leaner the mixture, the harder it is for a spark plug to ignite the air-fuel mixture. It takes a healthy ignition system in tip-top shape to ignite a very lean mixture (especially a LOP mixture) at high power. So to properly assess the health of the ignition system, we need to perform the mag check at high power and LOP. We call this an "ignition system stress test" because it's testing the ignition system under demanding conditions.

It's a bad idea to do this test on the ground because running the engine at high power is abusive unless there's plenty of cooling air flowing past the cylinder fins. We need to do this test in the air. Many pilots have never shut off a magneto in flight and are uncomfortable with the idea of doing so. That's too bad, because it's precisely what has to be done to gather the most valuable diagnostic data for troubleshooting ignition problems.

This chart shows a good example of an ignition stress test. Note how the #5 EGT goes unstable when the engine is running on the left mag only under high-power/lean-mixture conditions, indicating that the bottom spark plug in cylinder #5 has a problem. Also notice that all EGTs rise more during left-mag operation than during right-mag operation, suggesting that the two mags are timed differently (and they shouldn't be).

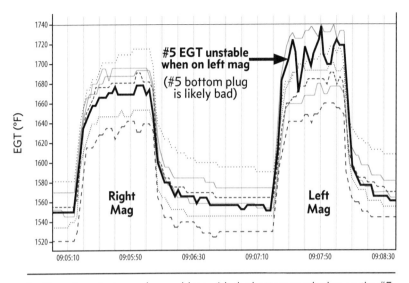

Ignition stress test reveals a problem with the bottom spark plug on the #5 cylinder, and also shows split ignition timing between the two mags.

I recommend performing the ignition stress test frequently. I do it on almost every flight, usually at the end of the cruise phase just before starting down. It should always be done any time any sort of engine anomaly is suspected in order to rule in or out an ignition system problem.

Mixture Distribution Test

Also known as the "GAMI lean test," the mixture distribution test determines how much mixture imbalance exists among the cylinders of your engine. In a perfect world, all cylinders would operate at precisely the same air-fuel mixture. But in the real world, there's always some variation in mixture among the cylinders—always some cylinders that are running a bit leaner and other cylinders that are running a bit richer. The difference in mixture between the leanest-running cylinder and the richest-running cylinder is called the "GAMI spread."

The GAMI lean test should be performed during cruise flight at a relatively low power setting (65 percent or below). It requires an engine monitor that displays/records EGT for each cylinder, and it also requires an accurate (preferably digital) fuel-flow gauge. Starting with a rich mixture, the mixture control is moved very, very slowly until the mixture is so lean that the engine starts to run quite rough. Each cylinder's EGT will rise to a peak value and then descend as the mixture becomes LOP. As each cylinder reaches peak EGT, the fuel flow is recorded. The cylinder that reaches peak EGT first (i.e., at the highest fuel flow) is the leanest cylinder, and the one that reaches peak EGT last (i.e., at the lowest fuel flow) is the richest cylinder.

The GAMI spread is simply the difference between those two fuel flows. We'd like it to be as small as possible—ideally zero, but of course that never happens. For a fuel-injected engine, we'd like to see the GAMI spread less than 1 gph, preferably less than 0.5 gph; if it's worse than that, we can usually reduce it by tweaking the fuel nozzles. For carbureted engines, the GAMI spread is often 2 gph or more.

It's usually best to repeat this procedure several times to ensure reliable results.

This test can detect dirty or wrong-sized fuel nozzles, intake valve problems, induction leaks, and other engine anomalies that can cause uneven mixtures among cylinders.

This chart shows a mixture distribution test that reveals a GAMI spread of 0.5 gph, which is quite good. Note that this engine monitor is configured to capture fuel flow information, making the analysis very easy and eliminating the need to record the fuel flow information manually.

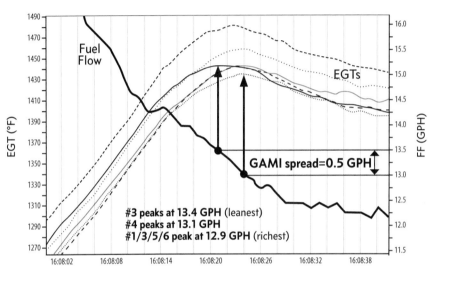

Mixture distribution test reveals an excellent GAMI spread of 0.5 gph.

I recommend performing this test every 12 months prior to putting the aircraft in the shop for its annual inspection. Also perform it any time any sort of engine anomaly is suspected in order to rule in or out a fuel system problem.

Detailed procedures for performing these flight-test profiles can be found on the SavvyAnalysis.com website.

So... Do You or Don't You?

If you don't have a modern recording digital engine monitor, I guarantee that you'll waste thousands of dollars paying mechanics to perform exploratory surgery to diagnose engine problems that could be diagnosed in minutes using engine monitor data. This is one piece of equipment that invariably pays for itself in short order.

Many owners have the impression that engine monitors are appropriate only for complex, high-performance aircraft and overkill for simple ones. In my view, that's bass-ackwards. The way I see it, if I lose a cylinder in my 12-cylinder, turbocharged twin, I continue to my planned destination and worry about how expensive it's going to be to replace the failed cylinder. If the same thing happens in a 6-cylinder single like a Bonanza, Saratoga, or P210, the result will be a precautionary landing at the nearest airport and a possible change of underwear. And if it happens in a 4-cylinder single such as a Skyhawk or short-wing Piper, the result might well be an off-airport landing.

So I ask you: Who needs good engine instrumentation the most?

If you do have a modern recording digital engine monitor and use it only for leaning, you may be missing out on its awesome potential as an engine health monitor and diagnostic tool. If you think you have an engine problem, your first move should almost never be to put your airplane in the shop and let a mechanic attack it with tools. It should be to dump your engine monitor data and either analyze it yourself or have it analyzed professionally.

Takeaway: Every piston aircraft should have a digital engine monitor installed, even simple low-performance aircraft. (Especially those.) This is technology that pays for itself very quickly. If you don't have one, you need one. If you have one, you need to learn to take advantage of its full potential as a condition-monitoring and troubleshooting tool.

6

The Dark Side of Maintenance

There's a dirty little secret about maintenance: It sometimes breaks airplanes instead of fixing them.

Have you ever put your airplane in the shop—perhaps for an annual inspection, a squawk, or a routine oil change—only to find when you fly it the first time after maintenance that something that used to work fine no longer does? I'll bet a steak dinner at Ruth's Chris that every aircraft owner has had this happen. I sure have.

Maintenance has a dark side that isn't usually discussed in polite company: Although the purpose of doing maintenance is ostensibly to make our aircraft safer and more reliable, the fact is that it sometimes accomplishes the opposite.

When something in an aircraft fails due to something that a mechanic did—or failed to do—we refer to it as a "maintenance-induced failure" or "MIF" for short. Such MIFs occur a lot more often than anyone cares to admit. Let's take a closer look.

What Makes High-Time Engines Fail?

I first started thinking seriously about MIFs in 2007, when I was corresponding with Dr. Nathan Ulrich about the causes of catastrophic piston aircraft engine failures, with particular emphasis on high-time engines operated beyond TBO. Dr. Ulrich did ground-breaking research on this subject by analyzing five years' worth of NTSB accident data, as I discussed in Chapter 3.

Dr. Ulrich's analysis showed conclusively that by far the highest risk of catastrophic engine failure occurs when the engine is young—during the first two years and 200 hours after it is built, rebuilt, or overhauled—due to "infant-mortality failures." However, the NTSB accident data was of little statistical value in analyzing the failure risk of high-time engines that are beyond TBO simply because so few engines are operated past TBO. We don't have any data on how many engines are flying beyond TBO, but we're pretty sure that it's a relatively small number.

So it should come as no surprise that the NTSB database contains very few accidents attributed to failures of over-TBO engines. Because there are so few, Dr. Ulrich and I decided to examine all such NTSB reports for 2001 through 2005 to see if we could detect some pattern of what made these high-time engines fail catastrophically. Sure enough, we did detect a pattern.

About half the reported failures of over-TBO engines stated that the reason for the engine failure could not be determined by investigators. Of the half where the cause could be determined, a whopping 80 percent were MIFs. In other words, those engines failed not because they were past TBO, but because mechanics worked on the engines and screwed something up!

Why Do MIFs Happen?

Numerous studies indicate that roughly three-quarters of accidents are the fault of the pilot. The remaining one-quarter are machine-caused, and those are just about evenly divided between ones caused by aircraft design flaws and ones caused by MIFs. Still, one-eighth of accidents is a pretty significant number.

The lion's share of MIFs are errors of omission. They include fasteners left uninstalled or untightened, inspection panels left loose,

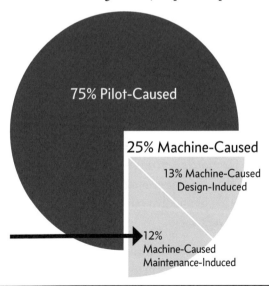

Causes of aircraft accidents.

fuel and oil caps left off, things left disconnected, and other reassembly tasks left undone.

Distractions play a big part in many of these omissions. A mechanic installs some fasteners finger tight, then gets a phone call or goes on lunch break and forgets to finish the job by torquing the fasteners. I have personally seen some of the best, most experienced mechanics I know fall victim to such seemingly rookie mistakes, and I know of several fatal accidents caused by such omissions.

Maintenance Is Invasive!

Any time a mechanic takes something apart and puts it back together, there's a risk that something won't go back together quite right, and the result will be a MIF. Some maintenance operations are more invasive than others, and the more invasive the maintenance, the greater the risk of a MIF.

When considering any maintenance task, we should always think carefully about how invasive it is, whether the benefit of performing the procedure is really worth the risk, and whether less invasive alternatives are available.

Many owners believe—and many mechanics preach—that preventive maintenance is inherently a good thing, and the more of it you do the better. I consider this a wrongheaded view. I think we often do far more preventive maintenance than necessary and we often do it using unnecessarily invasive procedures, thereby increasing the likelihood that our efforts will actually cause failures rather than prevent them.

In Chapter 2, I discussed reliability-centered maintenance (RCM) developed at United Airlines in the late 1960s, and universally adopted by the airlines and the military during the 1970s. One of the major findings of RCM researchers was that preventive maintenance often does more harm than good, and that safety and dispatch reliability can often be improved substantially by reducing the amount of preventive maintenance and using the least invasive methods possible.

Unfortunately, this sort of thinking doesn't seem to have trickled down to piston GA maintenance and is considered heresy by many mechanics because it contradicts everything they were taught in A&P school. The long-term solution is for GA mechanics to be trained about RCM principles. But that isn't likely to happen any time soon. In the short term, aircraft owners can improve the situation by thinking carefully before authorizing an A&P to perform any invasive maintenance procedure on their aircraft. When in doubt, get a second opinion.

Takeaway: The problem of maintenance-induced failures is huge. Every time maintenance is done — especially if it's invasive — it introduces the opportunity for a MIF to occur. The antidote is to do the absolute minimum amount of maintenance necessary to make the aircraft safe, reliable, and legal. Decline any work — particularly invasive work — that doesn't absolutely need to be done. Owners need to master the art of telling their mechanics "no, thanks."

7
How A&Ps Think

An A&P's decisions are rarely motivated by greed; they are much more likely to be motivated by fear—specifically, fear of the unknown and fear of getting sued.

If you've read this far, you know that I'm an unabashed maintenance minimalist. I believe in doing only the maintenance necessary to make an aircraft safe, reliable, and compliant with regulations. I am convinced that doing more maintenance than this is not only a waste of time and money but also makes the aircraft less safe and reliable.

This less-is-better maintenance philosophy has served me well for decades. It has become an established science called reliability-centered maintenance and has been widely adopted by airlines, military aviation, high-end bizjets, and industrial activities from nuclear powerplants to water treatment plants to offshore oil platforms.

But this less-is-better philosophy seems to be utter heresy to many GA mechanics who were taught in A&P school that maintenance is an inherently good thing, and that more maintenance is better. I deal with such maintenance maximalists daily in my managed-maintenance practice. I often wind up having some interesting discussions with these folks, and an occasional arm-wrestling match.

My managed-maintenance clients sometimes find themselves caught between the proverbial rock and a hard place—between their mechanics' maximalist recommendations and my minimalist guidance—and having to decide whose advice to take. It's fairly common for owners to start off following their mechanics' advice and then—after experiencing a series of scary and/or costly MIFs—coming around to my way of thinking.

I understand fully that the notion that doing less preventive maintenance makes an aircraft safer and more reliable is counterintuitive and hard to accept. Nevertheless, the evidence that it's true is compelling and incontrovertible to anyone willing to study the data.

Resistance to Change

For the first decade after I purchased my Cessna 310 in 1987, I used strictly Goodyear Flight Custom tires, which mechanics told me were the gold standard for GA aircraft tires. In 1998, I switched to Michelin Air tires because they were less pricey than the Flight Customs, but were rated for the same weight and speed and reported to last just as long. I had just as good luck with the Michelins as I did with the Goodyears.

Then, in 2005, I decided to try Desser retreads after *Aviation Consumer* did a big competitive torture test of various tire brands (Goodyear, Michelin, McCreary, Condor), and found that Desser retreads fared even better than top-of-the-line Goodyear Flight Customs, while costing half as much.

Are new tires (left) worth twice the price of retreads (right) that last longer?

I've used Desser retreads ever since, and *Aviation Consumer* was right: The darn things wear like iron. They're dimensionally identical to new tires, so there's never been any question about their fit in the wheel wells. Half the price, equal or better lifespan, perfect fit… what's not to like? Could this be why most commercial aircraft operators and flight schools use retread tires, as do virtually all airlines?

In 2008, I started recommending Desser retreads for my company's managed-maintenance clients. The reaction from shops and mechanics was astonishing. You'd have thought I'd just lit a stink bomb in church!

A number of shops flatly refused to install retreads, claiming they were taking this position "for liability reasons." Others reacted with contempt and derision: "You're serious about nickel-and-diming the maintenance by installing el-cheapo *recaps* on a half-million-dollar aircraft? Are you out of your mind?"

The fact that the biggest customers for retreaded aircraft tires are commercial operators, flight schools, and airlines didn't seem to carry any sway with these mechanics. Nor the fact that Desser retreads beat Goodyear's and Michelin's top-of-the-line new tires in the *Aviation Consumer* torture test.

Silly me. I always considered saving money a good thing. To paraphrase the late Senator Everett Dirksen, "A hundred bucks here, a hundred bucks there, and pretty soon you're talking real money."

Six years later, all of my clients who followed my advice and opted for retreads are very happy with their decision. Other clients demurred and sprung for the pricey Flight Custom IIIs. I have learned not to push the issue. I still use Desser retreads on my airplane.

Spark Plug Wars

In 2006, I needed to replace the spark plugs on my airplane. My twin has 24 plugs, so a full set of new plugs represents a non-trivial expense. While pricing out a set of Champion RHB32E massive-electrode plugs, I noticed that Autolite spark plugs were four bucks cheaper, a savings of $100 on 24 plugs. A hundred here, a hundred there…

I'd used nothing but Champion plugs for the past 35 years, but as a world-class cheapskate I just couldn't resist saving a hundred bucks, so I ordered the Autolites. When the new plugs arrived, I installed them and was very impressed. For one thing, the Autolite plugs are nickel-plated so they are much more corrosion-resistant than Champions (which are painted). For another, the Autolite threads start with a taper that makes them much easier to start in the cylinder spark plug boss. Subsequently, I learned that the Autolite plugs incorporated a fired-in sealed resistor assembly that solved the problem of high-resistance plugs that long plagued Champions.

Champion had dominated the aircraft spark plug market for as long as I could remember (and that's a long time), but these Johnny-come-lately Autolites (first introduced in 2002) were simply a better mousetrap. I've used Autolite plugs (which are now called "Tempest" after Unison sold the product line to Aero Accessories) ever since, and I love them. In 2008, I started recommending Autolite plugs to my managed-maintenance clients, and the blowback from their mechanics was truly breathtaking.

"My A&P was appalled that anyone would consider using Autolite plugs," one owner told me. "Since he's something of a curmudgeon, I asked my hangar neighbor (who's an A&P) and was treated to a tirade about how he once tried a set of Autolites and they all died after 150 to 250 hours. I then wandered to another FBO on the field to take a straw poll of the two A&Ps on coffee break and was treated like a dummy who would sacrifice my airplane to save a few bucks."

"I told my A&P this morning that I'd just installed Autolite plugs," another owner said. "It was like throwing gasoline on a barbecue. I got out of there very quickly."

Yet another owner received this inscrutable response from his A&P: "We like Champions, they're better—but we use Autolites in our rental fleet and haven't had any problems." Translation: "If you're paying for the plugs, we recommend the high-priced spread, but if we're paying for them, well..."

I've never had an aircraft owner report any problems with the Autolite/Tempest plugs. Several manufacturers have issued service bulletins calling for Champion fine-wire plugs to be removed from service because they fail so often. Continental Motors now ships their factory engines strictly with Tempest plugs instead of Champions. Yet still I find that few A&Ps in the field stock anything but Champion plugs, and a few still refuse to install Tempests even when their customers specifically request them.

Where's the Beef?

Why do so many A&Ps badmouth Desser retreads and Tempest plugs in the face of improved performance and cost-effectiveness? I've heard some owners suggest that it's because there's less mark-up on Desser tires than on Goodyears and on Tempest plugs than Champions. I'm not sure I buy that. In my experience, an A&P's decisions are rarely motivated by greed, and are much more likely motivated by fear—specifically, fear of the unknown and fear of getting sued. Besides, a genuinely greedy A&P could find much more lucrative outlets for his greed than spark plugs and tires.

This resistance to trying new things—a "late-adopter" mentality—seems disturbingly common among A&Ps in my experience. It's the same psychology that causes some mechanics to discount the benefits of borescope inspections (often because they don't own a borescope), spectrographic oil analysis, and digital engine analyzers (because they're never learned to interpret the results), and to blame most cylinder problems on lean-of-peak operation (because they've never studied combustion theory and don't realize that their Toyota runs LOP on the drive home from work).

Why are so many A&Ps skeptical of new-to-them products, methods and ideas? Why do so many choose to live life on the trailing edge of technology? Two reasons: lack of training and fear of being sued.

When I first earned my mechanic certificate (after having been a certificated pilot for 35 years), I was astonished to learn that the FAA has no regulatory requirements for an A&P to receive recurrent training of any kind. I found that shocking. If pilots have to go through recurrent training at least every two years, why doesn't a similar requirement exist for the mechanics who maintain our airplanes?

In 2005, the FAA finally amended Part 145 to require mechanics who are employed by FAA certified repair stations to undergo initial and recurrent training. But most A&Ps who work on our piston aircraft are not employed by a certified repair station, so they still are not required to get any recurrent training. And the recurrent training that repair station mechanics receive often tends to reinforce the old way of doing things rather than teaching them about new ones. As a result, it's not uncommon to find piston-GA mechanics whose knowledge is seriously stale and out-of-date.

Fear of being sued is also a serious deterrent to mechanics trying something new. Lawsuits against shops and mechanics once were rare, but they have exploded over the last two decades for reasons I discuss in the next chapter. The cost of defending such lawsuits can be ruinous for an individual mechanic or small business. Mechanics and shops have become very reluctant to try anything new or different, for fear it might come back to bite them in court.

I am certainly not suggesting that all piston-GA mechanics suffer from stale knowledge and a fear of trying new products and methods. The smartest and most talented A&Ps I know are information junkies and leading-edge thinkers. But many mechanics are incredibly resistant to change, very reluctant to adopt new technologies and methodologies, and their opinions often lack any basis in actual hard data. Owners are wise to seek expert second opinions rather than accepting their mechanics recommendations as gospel.

Takeaway: It can take real work for an aircraft owner to find a mechanic who is willing to consider new products and modern maintenance methods, but it's worth the effort.

8

A Mechanic's Liability

If your mechanic seems over-cautious and self-protective in his approach to maintaining your airplane, he has good reason.

Mechanics have always been subject to FAA sanctions: certificate suspension or revocation, fines, warning notices, letters of correction, and remedial training. But during the 1960s and 1970s—the heyday of piston general aviation—such enforcement actions against GA mechanics were exceedingly rare. That's no longer the case.

In 1978, the FAA added a new rule (FAR 43.12) making it a violation for any mechanic to "make, or cause to be made, any fraudulent or intentionally false entry in any record or report that is required to be made, kept, or used to show compliance with any requirement under this part [of the FARs]."

In plain English, 43.12 makes it a violation for a mechanic to "autograph a lie"—to "pencil whip" a logbook entry, maintenance release, yellow tag, etc. If a mechanic signs a logbook entry stating that some airworthiness directive (AD) was complied with, or some other inspection or repair was performed and the FAA discovers that the work wasn't actually done as documented, the mechanic is toast.

The penalties for violating 43.12 are extraordinarily severe. An individual mechanic accused of violating it almost certainly faces revocation of all his FAA certificates and will likely be looking for a new career. A repair station can face daunting fines up to $250,000 per violation and/or revocation of its repair station certificate.

That said, it's not all that difficult for a mechanic to avoid getting in hot water with the FAA. The regulations that govern GA mechanics (Part 43) are vastly more concise and understandable than the ones that govern GA pilots and aircraft owners (Parts 91 and 135). In fact, Part 43 contains just 13 rules and they're remarkably straightforward.

Reduced to its bare essentials, Part 43 simply requires that a mechanic:

- Perform work "by the book" per manufacturer's instructions or FAA guidance.

- Use the proper tools per manufacturer's recommendations or industry practice.

- Do all work in such a fashion that the aircraft is safe to fly, conforms to its type design, and complies with all applicable ADs and airworthiness requirements.

- Record all his work in the aircraft maintenance records accurately.

- Be supervised when he does work he's never done before.

Pretty commonsense stuff, right? A mechanic who makes a good-faith effort to follow these basic rules is very unlikely to get in trouble with the Friendlies.

Civil Liability

But a mechanic who follows the FARs to the letter isn't out of the woods. If an aircraft he works on winds up in an accident, the mechanic may easily find himself hauled into court as a defendant in a civil lawsuit, accused of negligence for allegedly performing improper maintenance, and facing ruinous money damages and legal expenses.

Under tort law, there's no need to show that a mechanic violated a regulation in order to find him negligent. It is only necessary to convince a jury that he "failed to exercise such care as would be reasonably expected of a prudent person under similar circumstances," either by doing something a prudent mechanic would not do or by failing to do something a prudent mechanic would do. It's not necessary to prove this "beyond a reasonable doubt," but only by "a preponderance of the evidence"—in other words, the jury need only conclude that it's more likely than not that the mechanic acted negligently.

This "prudent mechanic" standard can be mighty fuzzy. Suppose, for example, the plaintiff's attorney representing the widow of an air crash victim alleges that a mechanic who worked on the aircraft was negligent because he failed to comply with a mandatory service bulletin (SB). We all know that there is no FAA requirement for a Part 91 owner to comply with SBs (even so-called mandatory ones) unless the SB is explicitly mandated by an AD. In fact, most Part 91 operators don't comply with most SBs.

Can a mechanic be found negligent if he doesn't comply with a SB? Would a prudent mechanic have complied with the SB? What if the mechanic recommended that the SB be complied with but the aircraft owner said no? How would a jury of citizens who have no background in aviation, aircraft maintenance, or FARs decide these questions?

If you're an A&P, this is the stuff that keeps you awake at night.

The GARA Effect

In the salad days of piston general aviation, lawsuits against GA mechanics and shops were rare, because few GA mechanics and shops had enough assets to make them worth suing. Manufacturers like Beech, Cessna and Piper had deep pockets and insurance, so they were the primary targets of air crash litigation. Even if the cause of the crash seemed unrelated to the hardware (as is usually the case), the manufacturer would be sued anyway and would often wind up settling rather than incur the costs of going to trial.

Things changed dramatically 20 years ago when President Clinton signed into law the *General Aviation Revitalization Act of 1994* (GARA), which immunized GA aircraft manufacturers against product liability for aircraft older than 18 years.

There are a few exclusions from this immunity, but for the most part GARA provides the manufacturer with bulletproof immunity against air crash lawsuits.

Taking GA aircraft manufacturers off the hook didn't make air crash lawsuits go away. It simply increased the liability burden for everyone else involved with the accident aircraft, including engine and component manufacturers, aircraft owners, and *especially* mechanics and maintenance shops. In the wake of GARA, there has been an explosion of civil suits against maintenance folks.

This litigation explosion created another problem: Liability insurance for mechanics and shops has become hard to obtain. Many underwriters abandoned the maintenance market, leaving maintainers with few choices and little competition. Small shops and most individual mechanics are now forced to "go bare" and those lucky enough to be able to find insurance often pay exorbitant premiums for low coverage limits.

Nightmare Scenario

To illustrate the risks shops and mechanics face, consider the following hypothetical scenario created by aviation attorneys Stuart Fraenkel and Doug Griffith and derived from a composite of actual air crash lawsuits:

Peter Pilot of Charlie's Charter Service Inc. is flying passengers in a 1979 Cesscrafter 780 on leaseback from Oscar Owner and maintained by Mike Mechanic of Pristine Repair Corp. During an approach in IMC while being vectored by ATC, Peter Pilot is twice observed deviating from assigned altitude and heading and has to be given corrections. Shortly thereafter, the airplane enters a spin and crashes, killing all on board. Witnesses tell NTSB investigators that they heard the engine sputter.

Investigators find that Peter Pilot's medical expired a month before the crash. The toxicology report showed the presence of antihistamine medication in his blood. The airplane's tail section is located about 100 yards from the main wreckage, and its maintenance records indicate that Mike Mechanic of Pristine Repair Corp. had overhauled the airplane's engine 120 hours prior to the accident, but at the direction of Oscar Owner did not comply with one of the engine manufacturer's mandatory service bulletins.

Eighteen months later, the NTSB issues its probable cause determination: Peter Pilot suffered spatial disorientation while in IMC and lost control of the aircraft. A contributing factor was Mr. Pilot's use of an over-the-counter cold medication.

The families of the deceased passengers file a civil lawsuit. Defendants include the estate of Peter Pilot, Charlie's Charter Service, Mike Mechanic, Pristine Repair Corp., Oscar Owner, Cesscrafter, and the U.S. Government (who provided ATC services). In pretrial motions, the judge dismisses the suit as to defendants Cesscrafter (because of GARA) and the U.S. Government (because the controller's actions were deemed to be immunized under the "Discretionary Function" exception to the Federal Tort Claims Act).

The plaintiffs demand a jury trial. By law, the findings of the NTSB investigation and the probable cause determination are inadmissible at trial, so the jury never hears about them. The jury returns a judgment for the plaintiffs in the amount of $10 million, and allocates fault as follows: 10% to Peter Pilot and his employer Charlie's Charter Service; 10% to Mike Mechanic and his employer Pristine Repair Corp.; and 80% to Oscar Owner. Oscar's $1 million aircraft liability policy is limited to $100,000 per person.

This does not mean that Mike Mechanic and Pristine Repair Corp. are responsible for only $1 million, however. State law generally provides for "joint and several liability" for economic damages, which means that all defendants are equally liable to the plaintiffs to satisfy the entire amount of the $10 million judgment. Conceivably, the plaintiffs could come after Mike Mechanic and Pristine Repair Corp. for the entire $10 million, and leave it up to them to go after the other defendants for their share.

Is it any wonder that so many A&Ps and shops seem over-cautious and self-protective in their approach to maintenance these days?

The A&P's Dilemma

In the good ol' days before GARA, an A&P's maintenance decisions were guided by two principal concerns: (1) Is it safe? (2) Is it legal under the FARs? Those are precisely the two considerations a mechanic *should* be concerned about.

But in today's litigious climate, the prudent A&P is now forced to worry about a third concern: (3) How will it appear to a civil jury that knows nothing about aviation after being spun in the worst possible light by a skilled plaintiff's attorney? That is a very different standard indeed, and has had a tremendous chilling effect on A&P maintenance decision-making. Consider this scenario:

> *An owner brings his Cessna 182 to an A&P, complaining of nose-wheel shimmy. The mechanic investigates and discovers that the cause of the shimmy is that the bolt holes in the nose landing gear trunnion are worn, elliptical, and sloppy. The mechanic must now decide how to fix the problem.*
>
> *A new trunnion from Cessna costs more than $5,000. A used serviceable one from a salvage yard is available for half that price. The mechanic also considers the possibility of reaming the worn holes in the original trunnion oversize and installing bushings to restore the holes to their original dimensions; Cessna hasn't approved this*

repair, but the mechanic believes that it would fix the shimmy and be a minor alteration conforming to acceptable industry practices.

The A&P considers all three repair options to be safe and legal. But he worries what might happen should the airplane ever be involved in a nose-gear collapse and the mechanic finds himself in court. If the mechanic repairs the existing nose strut with bushings, a plaintiff attorney might ask him to explain to the jury why he made a repair that wasn't authorized by Cessna. If he replaces the damaged trunnion with a salvage yard part, a plaintiff attorney might ask him to explain to the jury why he decided to install "an undocumented part from a junkyard."

If you were the A&P, what would you do?

A&Ps face such dilemmas all the time: What about an engine that is past TBO that the owner wants to continue in service because it's running great? How about a costly SB that the owner doesn't want to comply with? The mechanic may believe that keeping the engine in service or ignoring the SB is both safe and legal, but is understandably worried whether such actions might not appear reasonable and prudent to a jury of aviation-challenged citizens, especially after the plaintiff lawyer makes them sound like capital crimes.

A Solution?

The obvious solution to this dilemma is that aircraft owners shouldn't put their mechanics in situations like this. The decision-making burden should rest with the owner, not with the mechanic.

Here's how this should work: The A&P informs the owner about Cesscrafter Service Bulletin 99-44 that calls for the frammis at the distal end of the portoflan armature to be replaced with an improved part, and explains that compliance with the SB will cost approximately $2,400. After consulting with a tech rep at the Cesscrafter Owners and Pilots Association, the owner decides he doesn't want this costly SB to be performed. The A&P then presents a signed-and-dated letter to the owner that says:

> I advised the owner of N12345 of Cesscrafter Service Bulletin 99-44. The aircraft is operated under Part 91, and therefore compliance with this SB is not required by regulation. After a thorough discussion of the technical and regulatory aspects of SB 99-44, the owner decided that he did not want this work performed, and instructed me not to do it.

The A&P asks the owner to countersign a copy of this letter, acknowledging receipt, and keeps the copy in his files. Such a contemporaneous written record would almost certainly go a long way toward convincing a jury that the A&P was not negligent in failing to comply with the SB.

This doesn't solve all the A&P's liability concerns. Unless he is blessed with 20-20 foresight, the A&P can't anticipate every possible decision that might ultimately be used as a basis for an allegation of negligence. But he certainly can anticipate the obvious ones (like busting TBO or declining SBs and other manufacturer's recommendations), and for those this is an easy and effective antidote.

Some owners just don't want to get involved in the messy business of maintenance decision-making and expect their mechanics to make decisions on their behalf. They might even feel annoyed if their mechanic hands them a "CYA letter" placing the decision-making burden on them. That's fine so long as the owner understands that in today's climate, mechanics and shops can be expected to make decisions that minimize their perceived liability exposure, and that such decisions can be very costly for the owner.

Takeaway: Owners concerned with controlling maintenance costs simply must get involved in the process and be willing to accept responsibility for key maintenance decisions. If you let your mechanic make those decisions for you, you may not be happy with the outcome.

9

Owner-in-Command

Just as a pilot-in-command has direct responsibility and final authority for the operation and safety of a flight, an owner-in-command has direct responsibility and final authority for the maintenance and airworthiness of an aircraft.

Every pilot understands the notion of pilot-in-command (PIC) because our CFIs mercilessly pounded this essential concept into our heads throughout pilot training. As PIC, we are directly responsible for, and the final authority as to, the operation of our aircraft and the safety of our flight. Our command authority is so absolute that in the event of an in-flight emergency, the FAA authorizes us as PIC to deviate from any rule or regulation to the extent necessary to deal with that emergency. (14 CFR §91.3)

When a pilot progresses to the point of becoming an aircraft owner, he suddenly takes on vast additional responsibilities for which his CFI most likely did not prepare him. Specifically, he becomes primarily responsible for maintaining his aircraft in airworthy condition. (FAR 91.403) Unfortunately, few owners have had the benefit of a certificated ownership instructor (COI) to teach them about their daunting new responsibilities as owner-in-command (OIC).

Too many aircraft owners fail to comprehend or appreciate fully their weighty and complex OIC responsibilities. They put their aircraft in the shop, hand over their keys and credit card, and tell the mechanic to call them when the work is done and the airplane is ready to fly. Often, owners give their mechanics *carte blanche* to "do whatever it takes to make the aircraft safe," and sometimes don't even know what work is being performed or what parts are being replaced until after the fact when they receive a maintenance invoice.

In short, most owners seem to act as if their mechanic is responsible for maintaining the aircraft in airworthy condition. But that's just flat wrong—just as wrong as thinking that an air traffic controller is responsible for the operation and safety of a flight. It's the PIC who's primarily responsible for safety, and the OIC who's primarily responsible for airworthiness. The mechanic and controller are there to help out in a supporting role.

Who's in Charge?

The very essence of the OIC concept is that an aircraft owner needs to remain firmly in control of the maintenance of his aircraft, just as the PIC needs to remain firmly in control of the operation of the aircraft in flight. When it comes to maintenance, a proficient aircraft owner is the head honcho who makes the major decisions about what work is to be done or deferred, rides herd on time and budget constraints, and generally calls the shots. The mechanics and inspectors and repair stations he hires are *subcontractors* with special skills, training, and certificates required to do the actual work. But the owner must always stay firmly in charge because the buck stops with him, literally.

Since most owners have not received any training in how to perform as OIC, many are simply overwhelmed by the prospect of taking command of their maintenance. "I don't know anything about aircraft maintenance," they moan. "That's way outside my comfort zone. Besides, isn't that my mechanic's job?"

No, it isn't. It's the owner's job.

Some owners take the attitude that it's their job to fly the aircraft and the mechanic's job to maintain it. They leave the maintenance decisions up to the mechanics, and then get frustrated and angry when squawks don't get fixed, when maintenance invoices cause sticker shock, and when outcomes aren't what they expected.

Consider this: If you were remodeling your house and you told your plumber, electrician, roofer, drywall, or paving contractor, "just do whatever it takes and send me the bill when it's done," do you think you'd be happy with the result?

No one in his right mind would do that. You'd start by giving the contractor a detailed description of exactly what you want him to do. You'd then expect the contractor to come back with a detailed written proposal, including cost estimates and a completion schedule. You'd go over that proposal in detail and make any necessary revisions. Then, once you and the contractor were on the same page about the work to be done and the cost and schedule, you'd sign off on the proposal and only then would the work commence.

Or consider what happens when you take your car to the shop for service. Typically you start by having a discussion where you describe exactly what you want done while the shop manager or service writer takes detailed notes. Once the two of you arrive at a meeting of the minds about what work needs to be done and how much it will cost, the shop manager or service writer goes to his computer, prints out a detailed work order with specific cost estimates, and asks you to sign the approval block and to keep a copy of what you signed.

Aircraft Inspection Report and Repair Estimate

The following is the annual inspection report on your Beechcraft V35A N1234V. Estimates do not include freight charges. Please review and give me a call to discuss and authorize repairs.

NOTE: Items marked as "UNAIRWORTHY" are items that I feel must be corrected before I can approve the aircraft for return to service. Repair of other listed items is recommended but not required.

Thank you...Isaac Abernathy, A&P/IA (1-800-555-1212)

1. Annual inspection and service (flat rate)	$1,500.00
10 quarts Aeroshell 15W50 @ $5.10/quart	51.00
1 Champion CH48109-1 oil filter	26.55
Miscellaneous parts and shop supplies	25.00
TOTAL	$1,602.55
2. Oxygen cylinder beyond 24-year service life limit	
1 serviceable cylinder	750.00
4.0 hours to remove and install	320.00
Sales tax @ 7.50%	54.38
TOTAL	$1,124.38
3. RH fuel gauge stuck, fuel quantity transmitter leaking fuel (UNAIRWORTHY)	
1 overhauled/exchange transmitter	175.00
3.0 hours to drain fuel, install transmitter, refuel	240.00
Sales tax @ 7.50%	17.70
TOTAL	$432.70
4. Right main landing gear tire worn, flat-spotted	
1 6.00x6 8PR Goodyear Flight Custom III tire	244.00
.6 hour to install	48.00
Sales tax @ 7.50%	17.69
TOTAL	$309.69
5. Left fuel tank quick drain leaking fuel (UNAIRWORTHY)	
1 quick drain	25.00
3.0 hours to drain tank, access fuel bladder, install new drain, refuel	240.00
Sales tax @ 7.50%	1.81
TOTAL	$266.81
6. Cabin door hard to close	
1.0 hour attempt to adjust	$80.00
7. Starter motor sounds rough due to bad bearings	
1 overhauled/exchange starter motor	300.00
.5 hour to replace	40.00
Sales tax @ 7.50%	21.75
TOTAL	$361.75
8. Induction air box support clamp broken (UNAIRWORTHY)	$48.00
.6 hour to fabricate and install replacement clamp	640.00
excessive leakage past exhaust valve, confirmed w/borescope (UNAIRWORTHY)	1,200.00
tall cylinder if found unrepairable (worst case)	87.00
	$1,927.00

Aircraft owners should insist on receiving a detailed written work statement and cost estimate like this one before authorizing any mechanic or shop to perform repairs or install replacement parts.

Yet many aircraft owners routinely turn their airplanes over to a mechanic or shop with no detailed understanding of what work will be done, what parts will be installed, and what it's all going to cost. All too often, the owner only finds this out when he picks up the aircraft and is presented with an invoice. At that point it's way too late for the owner to influence the outcome.

It always amazes me when I see aircraft owners do this (and I see it every day). These are intelligent people, usually successful in business (which is what allows them to afford an airplane), who would normally never consider purchasing goods or services without first knowing exactly what they are buying and what it will cost. Yet they routinely purchase aircraft maintenance without knowing either. Or even asking!

Often the result is sticker shock, bad feelings, and unpleasant owner/mechanic disputes that wouldn't have happened if only the owner had made sure he and his mechanic were on the same page to begin with. But once the work is done and the invoice presented, it's too late. You can't un-break an egg; you've got to prevent it from breaking in the first place.

Trust but Verify

Not a week goes by that I don't hear from disgruntled aircraft owners who are angry at some mechanic or shop. When I ask why they didn't insist on receiving a detailed work statement and cost estimate before authorizing the shop to work on their aircraft, I often receive a deer-in-the-headlights look followed by some mumbling to the effect that, "I've never had a problem with them before," or, "You've got to be able to trust your A&P, don't you?"

Sure you do…and you've got to be able to trust your electrician, plumber, and auto mechanic, too. But that's no excuse for not dealing with them on a businesslike basis. Purchasing aircraft maintenance services is a big-ticket business transaction and should be dealt with as you would deal with any other big-ticket business transaction. The buyer and seller must have a clear mutual understanding of exactly what is being purchased and what it will cost, and that understanding must be reduced to writing.

The most important factor that sets a maintenance-savvy aircraft owner apart from the rest of the pack is his attitude about maintenance decision making. Savvy owners understand that they have primary responsibility for the maintenance of their aircraft, and that A&Ps, IAs, and repair stations are contractors they must manage.

Takeaway: Savvy owners deal with aircraft maintenance professionals as they would deal with other contractors in other business dealings: They insist on having a written work statement and cost estimate before authorizing work to proceed. Then, like any good manager, they keep in close communication with the folks they've hired to make sure things are going as planned. If your mechanic or shop resists working with you on such a businesslike basis, you probably need to take your business elsewhere.

10

How to Manage Your Maintenance

During every annual inspection, there's a particular point in time when you and your IA need to sit down together and make decisions.

As an aircraft owner, you should never authorize any maintenance without first fully understanding the scope and detail of each proposed maintenance task to be done. Specifically, you need to know the answers to these questions:

- Why is this work being recommended?

- Is it an airworthiness issue?

- Is it required by regulation?

- Is it necessary for safety or reliability?

- How long will it take to accomplish?

- What will it cost?

- Are there any lower-cost alternatives?
- What's the worst that could happen if it isn't done now?

The annual inspection is generally the most difficult time for you to exercise management and oversight. It's difficult for two reasons: First, when you put your aircraft in the shop for an annual inspection, you have no idea what sort of discrepancies will be found during the inspection. So you have no way of anticipating the extent, time and cost of the work. Second, the aircraft is usually in the shop for quite a while at annual—typically a week or two, sometimes longer—and you probably have neither the time nor inclination to hang around the shop and oversee the work.

Despite these difficulties, the annual inspection is the most important time for you to exercise your management and oversight role. It's usually when the lion's share of your maintenance dollars are spent, and when there's the greatest risk of misunderstandings, surprises, ruffled feathers, aggravation, sticker shock, disputes, litigation and other nasty manifestations that often occur when owners let the maintenance process get out of control.

One obvious way for you to manage and oversee the annual inspection is to do an owner-assisted annual. In fact, I strongly urge every aircraft owner to go through this experience at least once during their aircraft ownership career because it's such a marvelous and invaluable education. (I got my own start in aircraft maintenance 25 years ago by participating in an owner-assisted annual, never suspecting where that might lead.)

But I recognize that most aircraft owners are not in a position to do owner-assisted annuals on a regular basis. So short of taking time off from work and camping out at the maintenance shop, how can you stay in control? Before answering that question, let's review what goes on during a properly managed annual inspection.

Anatomy of an Annual

There are eight distinct steps to an annual inspection:

1. Open up the aircraft to make it inspectable.
2. Inspect the aircraft's maintenance records.
3. Inspect the physical aircraft.
4. Create a list of discrepancies found during the inspection.
5. Repair the discrepancies.
6. Perform preventive maintenance.
7. Close up the aircraft to make it flyable.
8. Complete the paperwork (logbook entries and invoice).

The Decision Point

There is a crucial point in this process when you need to get involved. I call it "the decision point" because it's the point when critical decisions are made that affect what work will be done, what parts will be purchased, and what you will wind up paying to get the annual signed off and the aircraft back in the air.

The decision point occurs between step 4 (when the IA creates the discrepancy list) and step 5 (when the discrepancies are repaired). At this critical point in time, it is essential for you to sit down with the IA and go over the discrepancy list point by point.

You should require the IA to provide a detailed written estimate of what it will cost (both parts and labor) to correct each discrepancy, and you should discuss which items are airworthiness issues (that must be addressed right away) and which are discretionary items (that could be prudently deferred).

Discrepancy List and Cost Estimate for N313SR

Item Discrepancy	Corrective Action	Est. Labor	Est. Parts	Owner's Response	
1. MP sensor inop	Replace MP sensor	$171.50	$159.84	Approved	
2. NLG steering stiff	Replace spindle cup, bearings, Belville washers, and thrust washers	$514.50	$436.48	Declined	Owner has noted no steering issue
3. Fuel nozzle cleaning due each 300 hours	Clean fuel nozzles	$318.50	$10.62	Declined	GAMI spread good per engine monitor
4. NLG rebound bumper dry rotted	Replace NLG rebound bumper	$73.50	$48.04	Approved	
5. L & R VOR antenna grommets on upper tail cracked	Replace antenna grommets	$122.50	$4.62	Approve	
6. NLG left fairing bracket cracked	Replace bracket	$73.50	$54.28	Approved	
7. Battery #2 due for replacement each 2 years	Replace battery #2	$147.00	$100.30	Declined	Will replace on-condition
8. Main & essential bus voltage fluctuations	Require 2.5 hours to troubleshoot	$220.50	$0.00	Declined	Voltages are stable per engine monitor
9. Flight director bars do not respond to pitch movements	Recalibrate autopilot (requires flight test)	$258.75		Declined	Owner reports AP & FD "work like a charm"
10. Prop and governor due for overhaul due each 5 years	Overhaul prop and governor	$1,069.50	$0.00	Declined	Not required for Part 91 operator
11. Mfr-recommended overhaul/replacement items due each 5 years	Replace fuel vent flex lines, gascolator seals, fuel drain valve seals, flex brake lines, rudder-aileron interconnect shock cord	$2,205.00	$2,122.15	Declined	Will replace on-condition
12. TKS filter replacement due each 2 years	Replace TKS filter	$294.00	$218.00	Declined	Will replace on-condition
13. Engine induction air filter annual clean & service	Clean & service filter	$98.00	$0.00	Approved	
14. Magnetometer calibration due each 2 years	Calibrate magnetometer	$172.00	$0.00	Declined	Owner says heading indications accurate
15. Comply with TCM SID97-3 fuel system setup	Perform SID97-3 fuel system setup	$220.50	$0.00	Declined	No engine issues noted, TO FF good
16. Ignition harness springs corroded and deformed	Clean and adjust springs	$49.00	$0.00	Approved	
17. SOAP Oil Sample	Obtain oil sample	$14.70	$25.40	Approved	
18. Sealant worn on bases of Stormscope & COM antennas	Apply sealant	$171.50	$6.50	Approved	
19. NLG fairing cracked	Repair NLG fairing	$220.50	$20.50	Declined	Has been cracked for 3 years, stable
20. Recommend replace all _ drain seals	Replace all cylinder fuel drain seals	$230.00	$24.84	Declined	Will replace on-condition
	replace decals	$245.00	$24.02	Declined	Decals are legible
		$249.50	$74.32	Declined	No leaks noted

A typical discrepancy list and cost estimate from the shop, annotated by the owner with his decisions on which items are approved and which are declined.

At the conclusion of this "decision-point meeting" you and the IA should jointly agree on a plan of action, and be sure that you are on the same page concerning exactly what repairs will be made, what parts will be ordered, and what those repairs and parts will cost. Your decision about which repairs you wish to approve and which you wish to decline or defer needs to be put in writing so there's no possibility of confusion or misunderstanding.

There must also be a clear agreement by your IA that should unforeseen contingencies arise that could have significant impact on the agreed-to cost and schedule, the shop will stop work, inform you of the situation, and obtain your explicit authorization to proceed. That should be in writing, too.

It's usually best to accomplish this "decision-point meeting" face-to-face, but it can be done via e-mail or fax if necessary. However, don't do it over the telephone, because without a written record it's just too easy for miscommunication and subsequent finger-pointing to occur. Any time you communicate with your IA verbally, you should immediately memorialize the conversation in writing and provide your IA with a copy.

You need to make sure that your IA completes the inspection phase and has the "decision-point meeting" with you before any repairs are performed. Beware of the phenomenon I like to describe as "inspect a little, repair a little, lather, rinse, repeat." Some IAs like to make repairs as they go through the inspection, but when they do that it deprives you of a well-defined decision point and invariably you lose control of the situation. So it's essential for you to avoid this like the plague, and give your shop explicit instructions when you bring your aircraft in for its annual along the following lines:

"I'm authorizing you to open the airplane, perform the inspection and prepare the discrepancy list. Do not perform any repairs or order any parts until we go over the discrepancy list together and jointly decide on a plan of action. Please let me know as soon as you are ready for me to come in to do this, and make sure you have detailed written estimates prepared for each recommended repair and other maintenance items so I know how much each is expected to cost and can make an informed decision about what work to approve and what to decline or defer."

> ***Takeaway:*** Annual inspections and other maintenance events always should follow this well-defined three-phase protocol: (1) The mechanic inspects the aircraft and prepares a written discrepancy list for the owner, including repair recommendations and cost estimates; (2) The owner reviews the discrepancy list, recommendations and estimates, performs whatever due diligence is deemed necessary (including asking questions and seeking second opinions as needed), and then gives the mechanic detailed written instructions as to what work is approved and what work is declined; and (3) The mechanic performs the approved items as directed by the owner. If this protocol isn't followed, the owner invariably loses control of the process and is likely to be surprised by and/or displeased with the outcome.

11

Recommended or Required?

If an aircraft, engine, propeller, or appliance manufacturer prescribes maintenance, are you required to do it?

"It has been six years since your propeller was last overhauled, so we're going to have to overhaul it this year as required by Hartzell."

"Your magnetos are past due; Continental requires that they be overhauled every four years."

"We need to clean your fuel nozzles and adjust your fuel injection system annually—the maintenance manual says so."

I hear mechanics telling my clients these sorts of things every day. An important part of my job is to advise my clients to decline many of these things because (1) they're not required (even if the manufacturer says they are), and (2) doing them is often at best a waste of money and at worst a good way to create a problem where none exists. In my experience, many aircraft owners find it quite uncomfortable to say "no" to their mechanics and shops, so my clients look to me and my technical team to do that for them.

What is Required by Regulation?

Mechanics are often confused about exactly what maintenance is or isn't required by regulation, partly because the regulations are not terribly clear and partly because A&P training tends to be spring-loaded to the "always do it by the book" position. A large body of FAA Orders and Letters of Interpretation make it clear what the FAA's position is on this subject, but very few mechanics have ever read any of this stuff or received any training on the subject.

If you spend a little time studying this subject, it turns out that things are very simple, clear and unambiguous. Here it is in a nutshell...

Manufacturer's guidance comes in three basic forms: maintenance manuals (MM), instructions for continued airworthiness (ICA), and service bulletins (SB). It also comes in two basic flavors: "how-to's" and "when-to's." How-to's are the responsibility of mechanics and are covered in FAR Part 43; when-to's are the responsibility of aircraft owners and are covered in FAR Part 91.

The FARs refer to how-to guidance as "methods, techniques and practices" (MTPs). The general rule is that maintenance must be done in accordance with the MTPs specified in the manufacturer's MM or ICA or in accordance with other MTPs that the FAA finds to be acceptable. The specific regulatory reference is FAR 43.13(a), which states in pertinent part:

§ 43.13 Performance rules (general).

(a) Each person performing maintenance, alteration, or preventive maintenance on an aircraft, engine, propeller, or appliance shall use the methods, techniques, and practices prescribed in the current manufacturer's maintenance manual or Instructions for Continued Airworthiness prepared by its manufacturer, or other methods, techniques, and practices acceptable to the Administrator, except as noted in §43.16.

An exception to this rule is that how-to guidance that is set forth in an FAA-approved Airworthiness Limitations section (ALS) of a manufacturer's MM or ICA, which must always be followed exactly:

§ 43.16 Airworthiness limitations.

Each person performing an inspection or other maintenance specified in an Airworthiness Limitations section of a manufacturer's maintenance manual or Instructions for Continued Airworthiness shall perform the inspection or other maintenance in accordance with that section…

Although the FARs provide for using alternative acceptable MTPs (except for airworthiness limitations), such alternative methods are rarely available. So most of the time, mechanics wind up performing maintenance using the MTPs (how-to's) set forth in the manufacturer's MM, ICA and/or SBs.

What about "When-To's"?

"When-to" guidance includes manufacturer-specified inspection, overhaul, and replacement intervals, as well as other manufacturer guidance about how frequently various maintenance tasks are to be performed. Virtually every aircraft maintenance manual contains a long laundry list of scheduled maintenance tasks—things to be done every 50 hours, every 100 yours, every 12 months, etc. The maintenance manual for my Cessna 310 contains more than 250 such items.

Manufacturers of engines, propellers and appliances (e.g., magnetos, vacuum pumps, etc.) usually specify times between overhauls (TBO) or times between replacement (TBR) in MM or ICA or SBs. Lycoming, Continental, Hartzell, and McCauley all set forth their engine and propeller TBOs in service bulletins.

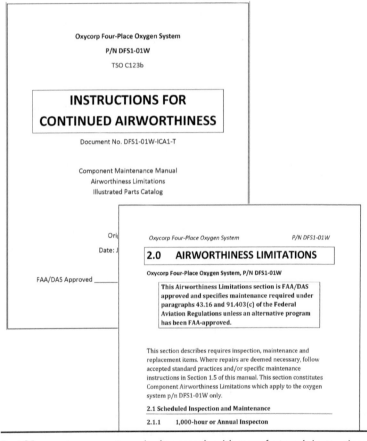

Part 91 operators are not required to comply with manufacturer's Instructions for Continued Airworthiness (ICA). They are only required to comply with the Airworthiness Limitations section contained in the ICA, if there is one.

As a general rule, Part 91 (non-commercial) operators are *never* required to comply with such manufacturer-specified intervals (when-to's). There's nothing in the FARs that states this explicitly. But there's nothing in Part 91 that requires compliance, either. Since the regs don't require it, you don't have to do it if you don't want to.

There are two—and only two—exceptions to this general rule: If inspection, overhaul or replacement intervals are mandated by an FAA airworthiness directive (AD) or if they are set forth in an FAA-approved ALS of the manufacturer's MM or ICA, then compliance is required by regulation. Otherwise, it isn't. The regulatory reference that covers these two exceptions is FAR 91.403, which states in pertinent part:

§ 91.403 General.
(a) The owner ... of an aircraft is primarily responsible for maintaining that aircraft in an airworthy condition, including compliance with Part 39 of this chapter [Airworthiness Directives].

(c) No person may operate an aircraft for which a manufacturer's Maintenance Manual or Instructions for Continued Airworthiness has been issued that contains an Airworthiness Limitations section unless the mandatory replacement times, inspection intervals, and related procedures specified in that section ... have been complied with.

Frequently Asked Questions

Q: Are you saying that I can ignore all of the scheduled maintenance tasks listed in my aircraft's maintenance manual?

A: If your maintenance manual has a clearly identified FAA-approved ALS, then any inspection, overhaul or replacement intervals prescribed *in that section* must be complied with. Intervals that appear in any other part of the maintenance manual need not be complied with. The maintenance manuals for "legacy aircraft" certificated under CAR 3 generally do not contain an ALS; those for newer-design aircraft certificated under FAR 23 typically do contain an ALS. The maintenance manuals for Lycoming and Continental engines do not contain any airworthiness limitations.

This doesn't mean you should ignore all manufacturer-prescribed maintenance intervals. Some of them make sense and are worth following, although many of them don't and aren't. Such intervals are simply recommendations, not requirements. You should feel free to accept or reject them as you see fit—except for ADs and airworthiness limitations, which are non-negotiable.

It makes no difference if the manufacturer uses compulsory-sounding words like "mandatory" or "required" or "must" or "shall." No manufacturer has the authority to compel you to perform any maintenance task that you don't want to do, regardless of what language the manufacturer uses. Only the FAA has that authority.

Q: Are you saying that I can ignore Instructions for Continued Airworthiness?

A: Yes, unless the ICA contains a clearly identified FAA-approved ALS. If it does, then any intervals prescribed *in the ALS* must be complied with. Intervals that appear in any other part of the ICA need *not* be complied with. Most ICA do not contain ALS, but some do.

Q: Are you saying that I can ignore service bulletins?

A: That's exactly what I'm saying. A Part 91 operator is *never* required to comply with any manufacturer's service bulletin— even those marked "mandatory" or "critical"—unless the FAA mandates compliance by AD. Again, I'm not saying that you should blindly ignore all SBs; some of them are quite important. I'm simply saying that whether or not you choose to comply with any particular SB is totally up to you—compliance is not required by regulation.

Q: Does this also apply to light-sport aircraft?

A: No it doesn't. The rules for light-sport aircraft (LSA) are completely different than the ones for certified aircraft. The FAA doesn't issue ADs against LSA, and they have no ICAs. The manufacturer of an LSA is the final authority on what maintenance must be done when, unlike certified aircraft where it's the FAA that's the final authority. If an LSA manufacturer says that something must be done in its MM or in an SB, then it must be done.

When to Say No

Learning when to say no to a manufacturer's or mechanic's maintenance recommendation takes a good deal of knowledge and experience, but there are a couple of basic rules. The most important rule is that you never say no to any maintenance procedure that is required by regulation. For example, Part 43 requires that every annual inspection on a piston aircraft must include a compression test of the cylinders, cutting open the oil filter to inspect for metal, and running up the engine to check that critical engine operating parameters (oil pressure, static RPM, etc.) are within normal limits. Mechanics are required to comply with any airworthiness limitations contained in the manufacturer's service manual or ICAs. Any applicable airworthiness directives must be complied with. All these things are non-negotiable.

It's also wise to avoid saying no to proposed repairs that the inspecting A&P/IA considers to be "airworthiness items." Those are generally discrepancies that he considers to be safety-of-flight items, and will not be comfortable approving the aircraft for return to service until they are corrected. When in doubt, you can try saying no and see how the IA responds. If he tells you he's not comfortable signing off the annual unless you approve the repair, then it's time to re-think your position.

Good candidates for saying no to include time-directed maintenance recommendations for things that can be readily done on-condition instead. Consider ignoring the time recommendations and replace or repair these items only when inspection shows that they need to be replaced or repaired. We should only be maintaining things on time (like the 500-hour magneto IRAN) if there's no practical way to maintain them on-condition.

Also consider saying no to preventive maintenance items intended to prevent failures whose consequences you consider acceptable. For example, replacing your vacuum pump every 500 hours (per the manufacturer's recommendation) is silly if you have dual vacuum pumps or a standby vacuum system or a backup electric attitude indicator. If a vacuum pump failure doesn't affect safety of flight, why not simply run it to failure and then replace it? Ditto if you have dual alternators or dual anything else.

Finally, consider saying no to overhauling anything if a simple repair will get the job done. (The official term-of-art is "inspect and repair as necessary" or IRAN.) Also consider saying no to replacing anything that can be repaired (unless a new one is so inexpensive that repair just isn't worth the trouble).

The art of saying no is definitely an acquired skill, but one that can save you a small fortune in reduced maintenance costs once you get the hang of it. Like any acquired skill, practice makes perfect.

If you say no to your IA with respect to something that isn't a clear-cut airworthiness discrepancy, the IA will generally accept your decision (even if he doesn't agree with it). If your IA resists taking no for an answer, you probably should seek a second opinion from a recognized expert on the issue in question. Once you obtain an expert second opinion, if you're still unable to reach agreement with your IA about the issue, you always have the option of directing the IA to "sign off the annual with discrepancies" and then find another A&P to clear the discrepancy and get you back in the air. (This "nuclear option" is rarely necessary; my firm manages 500-plus annuals a year, and only has to resort to it once or twice a year.)

Takeaway: With few exceptions, manufacturer-prescribed inspection, overhaul, replacement and other maintenance intervals are recommendations, not requirements. Sometimes they're bad recommendations that are at best a waste of money and at worst hazardous to the health of your aircraft. Every owner needs to learn which are worth following and which should be ignored and declined.

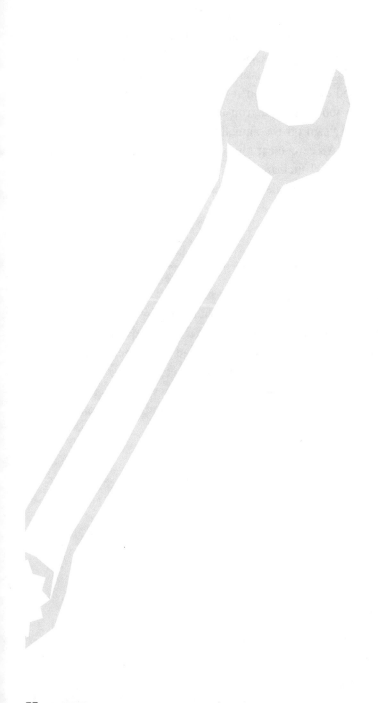

12
The Last Line of Defense

Never forget that on the first flight after maintenance, you're a test pilot. Act accordingly.

Part 91 contains a regulation about the first flight after mainte- nance, but it isn't terribly helpful:

§ 91.407(b) No person may carry any person (other than crew members) in an aircraft that has been maintained, rebuilt, or altered in a manner that may have appreciably changed its flight characteristics or substan- tially affected its operation in flight until an appropriately rated pilot with at least a private pilot certificate flies the aircraft, makes an opera- tional check of the maintenance performed or alteration made, and logs the flight in the aircraft records.

This regulation requires a test flight to be made (without passengers) after any maintenance to the aircraft "that may have appreciably changed its flight characteristics or substantially affected its operation in flight." But it leaves quite a bit to the imagination: Exactly what kind of maintenance meets this definition? Who makes the call whether or not a post-maintenance test flight (without pax) is required? How should the test flight be conducted? The regulation doesn't say.

One might think that a conscientious mechanic would counsel the owner to perform a post-maintenance test flight without passengers if the mechanic thinks it's necessary or required. In my experience, this almost never happens.

Furthermore, the fact that this regulation appears in Part 91 Subpart E (which speaks to aircraft owners) rather than in Part 43 (which speaks to mechanics) strongly suggests that the FAA considers it the responsibility of the owner, not the mechanic, to make the call as to whether a post-maintenance test flight needs to be made.

Certain kinds of maintenance—horsepower increase, speed mod, STOL kit, etc.—obviously require a post-maintenance test flight, since these alterations are specifically intended to "appreciably change flight characteristics." But what about an engine teardown or prop overhaul? An annual inspection? An oil change? Could these be expected to "appreciably change flight characteristics" or "substantially affect the aircraft's operation in flight"? In a perfect world, I suppose not.

But ours is hardly a perfect world. In our real world, mechanics and technicians make mistakes—lots of them! NTSB data clearly demonstrates the risk of a catastrophic engine failure on the first flight after a teardown or overhaul or rebuild is alarmingly high. Every pilot knows (or should know) that the first flight after maintenance is by far the most likely time for an equipment failure that can compromise safety of flight.

As we discussed in Chapter 6, maintenance-induced failures (MIFs) cause one out of eight aircraft accidents. Any time a mechanic takes something apart and puts it back together, there's a risk that something won't go back together quite right, and the result will be a MIF. Some maintenance operations are more invasive than others, and the more invasive the maintenance, the greater the risk of a MIF.

My own view is that a post-maintenance test flight should be made after *every* maintenance event, whether a "heavy annual" or a routine oil change. The test flight should be made without passengers, in day VFR conditions, and conducted in a safe environment in close proximity to an airport in case something goes wrong and the pilot needs to put the plane on the ground quickly.

Most important, it should be made with a *test pilot's mindset.* Start with an ultra-thorough preflight inspection performed as if your life depended on it (because it might). Then do an ultra-thorough runup that includes not only the usual mag check but also flight controls, avionics, autopilot, lighting, and every other system you can reasonably test on the ground. On takeoff, you should be spring-loaded to abort if anything looks, smells, sounds, or seems the slightest bit abnormal. Once airborne, you should be scanning the panel like mad and maintain heightened sensory awareness. Your expectation should be that something is probably going to go wrong before the test flight is over. At all times, be thoroughly skeptical that the airplane is airworthy. Hope for the best but be prepared for the worst.

Takeaway: The FARs don't require a test flight after every maintenance event, but to my way of thinking it's just common sense. I do it every time I swing a wrench on my own airplane. You should, too. It's your airplane. You are in charge of its airworthiness. No responsible pilot puts a trusting passenger in an untested airplane.

Epilogue

The minimalist, reliability-centered, data-driven, owner-directed maintenance philosophy described in this *Manifesto* arose out of a long personal journey. That journey involved more than 45 years as an aircraft owner and more than 25 years of being immersed in GA maintenance in one way or another. I now see that much of that time was spent reinventing the wheel, but I didn't realize it at the time.

Awakenings

I earned my private pilot certificate in 1965 while still an under-graduate at Dartmouth College majoring in mathematics. I bought my first airplane in 1968, a new Cessna 182 that I picked up at the factory in Wichita and flew home to California—heady stuff for a 24 year old. Four years later, my "need for speed" and desire for a sexier airplane caused me to trade in my Skylane for a new 1972 Bellanca Super Viking that I picked up at the factory in Alexandria, Minnesota. (Those were the crazy, boom days of GA when you could buy a new airplane and the U.S. federal government literally reimbursed you for half the purchase price in the form of tax credits and deductions.)

During my first two decades as an aircraft owner, I was the prototypical "appliance operator." I flew my airplane and let mechanics maintain it. I was a serious pilot who regularly flew transcontinental trips in serious IMC, and earned my commercial, CFIA and CFII. But pretty much all I knew about maintenance was that the process always ended with the receipt of a hefty invoice and the tendering of a credit card. At the time, that's all I cared to know.

I bought my third airplane in 1987. It was a 1979 Cessna T310R, my first used airplane, my first turbocharged airplane, my first airplane certified for flight in known icing, my first six-seat airplane, and, most significantly, my first twin. This represented a big step up in capability and a huge step up in complexity and maintenance intensiveness. With the benefit of 20/20 hindsight, I now see clearly it was far more airplane than I really needed and had entirely too many moving parts. I still own that airplane 27 years later—proof that I'm capable of irrational behavior—but if I was purchasing an airplane today, you can bet it would be a something vastly simpler like a Cirrus SR22 or perhaps even an RV-10.

Taking the Plunge

I still remember the first annual inspection of the 310 on my watch in late 1987. The very experienced IA who did the inspection wrote up a discrepancy list with nearly 100 items, and an invoice with a bottom line north of $10,000. (That's 1987 dollars—equivalent to about $22,000 today.) I was numb.

When it came time for my 1988 annual, my IA had taken a job as a civilian contractor to the Air Force, and his replacement at my shop was far less experienced and a bit wet behind the ears. This made me nervous, so I decided it might be a good idea for me to hang around the shop and keep an eye on him while my airplane was undergoing its annual. The young IA foolishly said okay to this, so I did.

"Hang around and watch" soon morphed into "hang around and help" (owner-hindered annuals), and that soon morphed into "work while being watched" (supervised maintenance). I seemed to have an aptitude for working on airplanes. It was an enjoyable and refreshing contrast to my regular job as a software developer and entrepreneur who spent most waking hours working at a computer. Within a few years, I was doing virtually 100 percent of the maintenance on my complex, turbocharged, known-ice piston twin—under A&P supervision mostly of the "call me when you're done and I'll sign it off" variety. I did this for more than a decade under the tutelage of a half-dozen experienced, generous, patient, and kind A&P/IA mentors before I finally logged enough experience to qualify for my own A&P certificate and subsequently my IA.

Once I started doing my own maintenance, it became obvious that my airplane had far fewer squawks and was far more reliable than it had been before. This struck me as totally counterintuitive because I was a novice mechanic with hardly any maintenance experience and even less maintenance knowledge.

Ultimately I discovered the reasons things got better instead of worse when I started doing my own maintenance: First, since I was acutely aware of being a know-nothing novice mechanic and frankly petrified of screwing up and causing a MIF, I worked on my airplane at a snail's pace, constantly referencing the maintenance manuals and obsessively double- and triple-checking everything to make sure I hadn't forgotten anything. (My mentors would tease me about being the world's slowest mechanic, and I was guilty as charged.) Second, I frequently asked my supervising A&P to check my work, so there were often two sets of eyes looking at anything I did that was even modestly invasive. Third, my hangar was a distraction-free environment: There was no phone, no customers, no Snap-On Tools truck, roach coach, or UPS deliveries; it was just me, my airplane, my toolbox, and some Bach Brandenburg Concerto on the CD player.

At first, I pretty much followed maintenance manual recommendations to the letter. But when the engines reached TBO, they were running so well that I just couldn't stand the thought of tearing them down. I continued to fly the engines for another 500 hours, after which I had them overhauled for no particularly good reason other than that I still wasn't totally convinced that piston engine TBO is a nonsensical concept that should be completely ignored. After both engines were torn down, I paid a visit to the engine shop to survey the damage and was shocked with what I saw: After TBO plus 500 hours, virtually everything in the engine other than the cylinder valve guides was within .001-inch of new limits. The graybeard overhaul shop owner told me that those engines could easily have run another 1,000 hours without breaking a sweat. As far as I was concerned, that was the final nail in the coffin for the TBO concept.

Over the years that followed, I started questioning the validity of other manufacturer-prescribed maintenance recommendations and started vetting them by asking myself, "What's the worst that could happen if I don't do this?" For the majority of recommended maintenance tasks, the answer was, "Nothing that would affect safety-of-flight or leave me stranded."

Hmmm.

I consulted with my mentors about the wisdom of ignoring those recommendations and got responses like, "Well, I probably wouldn't bother doing that if it were *my* airplane, but of course for a *customer's* airplane it would be a different story." Message received. I stopped performing those tasks that failed to pass through my "worst that could happen" filter. The result: Squawks became less frequent, dispatch reliability improved, and I spent fewer hours working in my hangar.

I was learning. I was becoming a dyed-in-the-wool maintenance minimalist.

Paying It Forward

Most of my mentors worked with the Cessna Pilots Association (CPA). They seemed to think I had an aptitude for troubleshooting airplanes and explaining complicated maintenance issues in language aircraft owners could grasp. (I attribute the former to my training in rigorous and abstract thinking as a mathematician and software engineer, and the latter to the fact that I was an aircraft owner for decades before I got involved in maintenance.) I was drafted as a volunteer technical representative for CPA. Over the next 20 years I had the privilege of helping thousands of Cessna owners solve their thorniest aircraft problems, mostly ones that had their local A&Ps stumped. Later, I volunteered to do similar work for the American Bonanza Society (ABS) and the Cirrus Owners and Pilots Association (COPA). It was an awesome learning experience.

I'd been a prolific aviation writer since 1970, but by the mid-'90s the focus of my writing shifted from flying to maintenance, partly because I was learning things about maintenance that I wanted to share, and partly because hardly anyone else was writing on the subject other than Kas Thomas's *TBO Advisor* newsletter. When Kas ceased publishing his newsletter a few years later, I found myself pretty much the only voice crying out in the wilderness of GA maintenance. Between 1995 and 2014, I authored more than 300 maintenance-related, feature-length articles in CPA magazine, ABS magazine, Cirrus Pilot magazine, AVweb (which I co-founded in 1995), *EAA Sport Aviation* magazine, AOPA Opinion Leaders Blog, and various other publications.

In 2004, I developed a 17-hour total-immersion maintenance seminar for aircraft owners and took it on the road at venues throughout the U.S. (and once in Australia). Over the next six years, more than 1,000 aircraft owners graduated from this seminar. But by 2010, the cost of putting on these live seminars became so oppressive that I ceased doing them, and instead started doing monthly online maintenance webinars co-sponsored by EAA. The webinars proved to be an awesome delivery vehicle. I had to charge $500 tuition for the live seminars, generally attended by 20 to 30 aircraft owners, but my monthly webinars draw 400 to 800 aircraft owners every month (and are viewed as videos by thousands more) and the tuition is free!

In the course of putting on those seminars for aircraft owners, I discovered that some of my graduates became excellent owner-in-command maintenance managers, but most didn't. Some just didn't have the time or inclination to get involved in the maintenance of their aircraft. Many lacked the necessary assertiveness to give direction to their mechanics (instead of the other way around). Although most of them were hard-driving, well-compensated professionals, executives, and entrepreneurs who were generally "masters of their domain," when it came to aircraft maintenance they were way outside of their comfort zone. It became clear that many would much rather be able to hire an expert to manage their maintenance than to learn to do it themselves. So in 2008, I founded Savvy Aircraft Maintenance Management, Inc. (SavvyMx.com) to provide professional maintenance management service for GA aircraft. As of 2014, Savvy manages the maintenance of more than 500 owner-flown aircraft in a dozen countries, including 10 percent of the U.S. Cirrus fleet.

Lessons from History

At first, it felt as if I was the only one in aviation preaching about the benefits of maintenance minimalism: ignoring TBOs, performing maintenance strictly on-condition, using minimally invasive techniques, and generally adopting an "If it ain't broke, don't fix it" philosophy. Then, in 2007, I received an e-mail suggesting that I might want to look into the work done in the 1960s by Stan Nowlan and Howard Heap at United Airlines. I paid $125 to acquire a copy of their 1978 report titled "Reliability-Centered Maintenance," devoured all 476 pages, and concluded that most of what I'd learned the hard way was stuff they'd discovered 40 years earlier. I subsequently bought two RCM textbooks—one by John Moubray (*Reliability-Centered Maintenance*) and the other by Anthony Smith and Glenn Hinchcliffe (*RCM: Gateway to World Class Maintenance*)—and read them cover-to-cover. I became more convinced than ever that my minimalist, condition-based approach to maintenance was the right one, and that there was a huge body of scientific research supporting that approach. But nobody in the world of owner-flown GA seemed to know about it.

In 2010, an aircraft owner named Colleen Keller, whose day job was doing mathematical analysis for the Department of Defense, e-mailed me a copy of an obscure article in the current issue of *Phalanx*, the journal of the Military Operations Research Society. The article was written by Dr. James P. Ignizio of the University of Texas (Pan American) and was lyrically titled "The Waddington Effect, C4U-Compliance, and Subsequent Impact on Force Readiness." (Huh?) In his article, Professor Ignizio made reference to a long-out-of-print 1973 book by the eminent British scientist C.H.

Waddington titled *Operational Research Against the U-Boat*. I was able to locate a slightly used copy at a rare bookseller in England, and it's now one of my prized possessions. The book described research done during the early 1940s by Professor Waddington and a group of scientists attached to the Royal Air Force that resulted in drastic improvements to the reliability and force readiness of squadrons of B-24 submarine-killer bombers achieved by slashing the amount of routine scheduled maintenance performed on those aircraft. Waddington's pioneering research into the benefits of maintenance minimalism remained classified until 1973 and was virtually unknown in the U.S. before 2010.

It seems that the compelling benefits of maintenance minimalism keep getting rediscovered every few decades. When will the word trickle down to GA mechanics?

What's Next?

Now that I've finally finished this *Manifesto*, I'm hard at work creating the remaining books in this multivolume set. The books will be anthologies of the hundreds of articles I've written over the past 25 years about engines, airframes, aircraft ownership, and flying.

Meantime, lots of exciting things are happening at Savvy. Our SavvyMx managed maintenance program has been growing by leaps and bounds. We launched a nationwide SavvyPrebuy service to help prospective aircraft buyers with pre-buy examinations of purchase candidates located anywhere in the U.S.

In 2012, we launched a new service called SavvyAnalysis offering the world's most sophisticated platform for archiving and analyzing piston aircraft digital engine monitor data (it's free!), and SavvyAnalysis Pro service where we provide expert analysis of engine monitor data for a modest fee. We now have more than

600,000 flights in our database, and created a "Savvy Skunk-works" to do basic research into how GA pilots are operating their engines in the real world.

Our first Skunkworks project is called FEVA—an acronym for Failing Exhaust Valve Analytics—that automatically detects the signature of failing exhaust valves on flights uploaded to the SavvyAnalysis platform, and immediately alerts clients and suggests they have a borescope inspection done to confirm the failing exhaust valve diagnosis. Our next Skunkworks project is a Savvy Report Card that will analyze key engine operating parameters (such as CHT, percent power, and leaning technique) that affect engine reliability and longevity, and will advise clients of how they're doing in comparison to other aircraft of the same aircraft or engine make and model.

We have a lot more ideas about how to drag GA maintenance kicking and screaming into the 21st century. Stay tuned!

—Michael D. Busch
  mike.busch@savvyaviator.com

Made in the USA
Columbia, SC
10 October 2024

44144562R00063